Customer, LLC

THE SMALL BUSINESS GUIDE
TO CUSTOMER ENGAGEMENT & MARKETING

HILLARY BERMAN

Customer, LLC: The Small Business Guide to Customer Engagement & Marketing

Copyright © 2016 by Hillary Berman

Library of Congress Control Number: 2016941788
ISBN: 978-0-9975996-0-2

Printed in the United States of America.

Editing: Monika Jansen
Cover Design: Alston Taggart
Covert Art: Ilana Graf
Interior Design: Emma Knight
Interior Photography: Paul Jones

CONTENTS

Section 3 – Getting Beyond Your List

Section 4 – So, Now What? Making It All Happen

FOREWORD

ANOTHER SMALL BUSINESS MARKETING BOOK?
WHY CUSTOMER, LLC?

Amazon and Barnes & Noble are overflowing with books on small business marketing and there are just as many on creating a strong referral culture. These books are fabulous, inspiring and full of examples of big brands that small businesses can theoretically emulate. If you're reading this, you've likely heard many times over about the amazing customer-centric culture at Zappos. Or how Uber went from a cool app to a national phenomenon seemingly overnight through an incredible viral referral program. Or anything about Disney – they've thought of everything!

But I often hear from many small business owners that it's hard to connect the dots between what big brands are doing and what they can – or should – do. While exciting, the big business case studies feel out of reach when working on a shoestring budget and three minutes a day dedicated to marketing.

Like other books out there, *Customer, LLC* contains many anecdotes and case studies to provide both inspiration and caution. But unlike the others, this book contains only stories about small businesses.

You'll read about a photographer creating amazing engagement with clients through manicures, and you'll learn about how magnets contributed to the demise of a local popcorn shop. Some stories showcase businesses doing something noteworthy and creative to connect with their customers, while others offer perspective on lessons learned the hard way when a business fails to consider the customer.

You'll also read about my own personal experiences with small businesses and stories shared with me by others.

(One note, when I highlight the not-so-great, I do so anonymously. Entrepreneurship and small business ownership are hard, and we all make mistakes. I'd never shame another small business owner for a mistake, and for that reason, I don't identify them by name or company.)

I also hear small business owners gripe about how big businesses can do more because of their size and resources – money, people, skills, you name it. But the thing is, as small businesses, we have a tremendous advantage over the big guys – agility. Being small means decisions can be made faster and ideas can be put into action for a significantly lower cost. This book offers ideas for small tweaks to your marketing and marketing mindset that offer big returns.

Today's customer is busier and more distracted than ever. And we live in an on-demand, "need" instant solutions world. Plus, customers have more options than ever. They can buy online from someone who never would have been your competitor 10 years ago. They're comparing prices while standing in your store. So effective marketing that empowers long-term, sustainable business growth requires more than a flash sale or jumping from the latest social media gimmick to the next.

When it comes to creating loyal customers, everything old is new again. It's time for a back-to-basics approach to customer service. Handwritten notes. A cup of coffee. A quarter for a customer's meter. It's about the little touches. Those are the ones that make a business memorable.

But the little things alone aren't enough. It's time for small businesses to move from "customer engagement" and "customer experience" as buzz words and strategies to an integral way of doing business. It's possible. And when customers are at the core of a business, the notion of "the customer is always right" is trumped by a business-customer relationship that both the business and the customer value.

Customer, LLC will provide you with perspective on how to achieve growth in your business. It encourages you to think about what your customer needs before you think about what you sell. And it guides you toward shifting how you think about your business and your marketing so your customer is at the center of your decision making and operations. A customer-centric business is a mindset. It's a way of looking at your business that leads to customer satisfaction, loyalty, referrals and growth.

Customer, LLC is divided into four sections, each of equal importance.

The Customer-Centric Mindset

What's the point of outbound marketing campaigns if you send would-be customers to a website with outdated information? The notion of "Check out our website for more info, but <insert embarrassed grin> we're working on it so please call me if you have questions!" simply won't fly. This section covers the key elements of getting your business set up for successful engagement and effective campaigns.

Customer-Centric Communications & Engagement

Start with the customers you already have – how can you deepen your relationships so they become repeat buyers and sing your praises? Existing customers are the best source of future business. This section outlines ways to engage both day-to-day and in more special ways that will really get them talking.

Getting Beyond Your List

Too many small businesses target their existing audiences over and over again. At some point, customers max out – there's only so much they need (or can be convinced) to buy. But which of the many, many marketing options are right for your business? This section helps break it down.

Now What? Making It All Happen

Excited and ready to turn up the heat on engaging with customers and marketing your business? Not sure where to start? It doesn't have to be overwhelming. This section guides you toward building your most awesome, customer-centric business possible.

So, onward! Get reading. Get inspired. Start engaging.

Section 1

THE CUSTOMER-CENTRIC MINDSET

Chapter 1

Defining Customer-Centric

A quick online search for "small business marketing" delivers pages of articles, dozens of top 10 lists, and hundreds of must-do tactics. While these easy-to-implement tips and tricks sound great in a vacuum, in reality, there's no quick fix.

Today's customers are bombarded with marketing messages at every turn. And they're trying to juggle these alongside their never-ending to do lists at home and work, the 24-hour news cycle, and taking care of everyone's needs – kids, spouse, parents and friends. And somewhere in there they're attempting to eat healthy, exercise, sleep, and potentially have five minutes for themselves.

All of a sudden, your perfectly crafted Facebook post that you paid to promote, complete with engaging photo, enticing offer and compelling call to action, doesn't compete with the myriad other demands on your customers. But if you're already deeply engaged with your customers, it can.

Being customer-centric is about making it easy for would-be customers to buy. It's about delivering a high-quality product or service consistently. Being customer-centric means making things right when the product arrives imperfect or the engagement doesn't go as planned. (It happens, even in the best businesses.)

A customer-centric business makes the customer priority number one and connects with them on a personal level – even through mass communications. And it's about knowing what makes customers tick. It's about being the kind of business that customers truly want to refer friends to, not only because they're incentivized to do so. A commitment to being customer-centric means putting customers' interests first.

Small businesses that thrive recognize their unique attributes and inherent strengths. They understand their market and competition. And they always keep their customer in focus – as they build and operate their business, sell and enhance their products/services, and promote and communicate their messages. They truly embrace their customers as the core of their businesses.

To be clear, being customer-centric does not mean you're not focused on selling. In fact, a customer-centric approach is all about sales. Yes, "sales." If ever there was a four-letter word (or five in this case) for business owners, "sales" is it. Like it or not, as a small business owner, you're always in sales. But sales isn't about going door-to-door or pushing a Tupperware party on everyone you know. This entire book is about sales. Being customer-centric is about making it easier to make sales.

Being customer-centric does not mean you sacrifice your business for the sake of customers. It does not mean that you compromise your core values, offer custom packages (unless that's already a part of your business model), or adjust pricing on the fly. If you do this, you'll spend all of your time satisfying no one. Rather, being customer-centric is about being a business that people want to buy from, refer to, and repeatedly come back to time and again.

Why is being customer-centric so essential? To understand that, we must first look at today's customer. We live in a world where customers can access products and information anywhere, anytime. They can be in your Main Street boutique and do a quick price check, get additional product (or competing product) information, and read product reviews from their phone. Suddenly you've lost a sale as they discover that they can purchase the same beautiful dress for 15% less on Amazon or that a more desirable, comparable product is available down the street. Customers might claim to want to support local business, but they also want to get the best price. The lesson? Make your buying experience and customer service worth it, price fairly (and match when you can) and consider loyalty programs. (There's more on pricing in chapter 7 and loyalty programs in chapter 15.)

"

Small businesses that thrive recognize their unique attributes and inherent strengths. They understand their market and competition. And they always keep their customer in focus – as they build and operate their business, sell and enhance their products/services, and promote and communicate their messages. They truly embrace their customers as the core of their businesses.

The access to information doesn't stop with retail and research. Today's customer is distracted in a nanosecond from your perfectly timed, beautifully worded, and flawlessly executed email campaign because the baby starts crying, a news alert pops up on their phone, or a thunderstorm breaks. Wait, what? Today's world is busy. Beyond the chaos in your customers' personal lives, anywhere, anytime access to email, social media and information is enough to make anyone's head spin. The lesson here is that while your one-day sale, awesome new service, or value-added content is top of mind for you, your customer must parse this information alongside every other detail of their day. So to stand out, it takes more than a monthly newsletter or Black Friday sale. It takes a top-to-bottom customer-centric approach to your business.

"

Being customer-centric doesn't take any more work than marketing in general. And it isn't any more expensive. Rather, it shifts the intention to being focused on the customer instead of only on your business.

To be fair, being customer-centric is hard. As a small business owner, you're entrenched in the day-to-day operations of running your business. You have to worry about everything from ensuring deliveries go out on time to fixing the broken faucet. And then there's dealing with the payroll company and hiring your next great employee. Somewhere in there you have to find time to develop your next awesome idea that will most certainly grow your business. And then there's marketing. How on Earth can you possibly think about your customer's perspective when it feels hard enough to get through your own thoughts each day?

Importantly, being customer-centric doesn't take any more work than marketing in general. And it isn't any more expensive. Rather, it shifts the intention to being focused on the customer instead of only on your business.

How do you know what your customers want? Ask! Happy, engaged customers are eager to join in your journey and provide perspective (you'll find more on feedback in chapter 13). And listen. Customers tell you in many ways without speaking the words. Do they open and click on links in your emails? Are they engaging with you on social media and tagging you in their posts? Are they buying your new products and sending you referrals? Mostly though, simply pause. Take a step back from your business and look at it again as an outsider. Would you buy from you?

THE BOTTOM LINE

Today's customer is hyper-connected and busier than ever before. As a result, your small business is up against not only your competition, but also the complexities and noise of everyday life. Being customer-centric makes it easier for a customer to connect with you and easier for them to buy from you. So consider their needs and their perspective as part of your decision-making process – it doesn't make marketing any more complicated or expensive, only more intentional and focused on building customer relationships.

Chapter 2

Building A Customer-Centric Foundation

You wouldn't build a house without pouring the foundation, right? So why do we as small business owners so often jump into "marketing" without first establishing the foundations of a customer-centric business?

"Marketing," as most business owners think of it, is the fun stuff – the videos that go viral, the awesome offers that drive hundreds of customers in a single week. "Marketing" is the social media, advertising, email campaigns, limited-time discounts and so on. "Marketing" is like the shiny, bright object, drawing out the toddler instinct in all of us. I think of my boys who, as babies, were instantly attracted to anything sharp, tiny and completely inappropriate for their stages of development. (To parents of the under two set, it doesn't get better. The shiny objects just get bigger, more expensive, and arguably more dangerous.) "Marketing" can be super enticing when building a business – and why not? On the surface, it drives new customers and reminds existing ones that you're out there and ready to deliver.

But without a strong foundation, "marketing" can quickly become an expensive, losing endeavor. And it can drive a potentially successful business out of business. So, as Maria von Trapp belted out in the Rodgers & Hammerstein classic, *The Sound of Music*, "Let's start at the very beginning, a very good place to start." Plus, it's time to drop the quotation marks that I know are making some of you insane.

Marketing (no quotes) includes everything it takes to secure a sale and to keep connected with a customer so they buy again. Marketing includes every interaction, whether in-person or indirectly via your website or storefront. Yes, this includes what is often typically referred to as "brand," but also everything else – how you define your products, how you price your offerings, how you communicate about what you sell, and, most importantly, how you engage throughout the customer lifecycle. All of these things contribute to the buying experience and customer engagement. While these areas might not feel like marketing and often aren't as fun as the campaigns we more often think of as marketing, a well-thought-out, customer-centric approach to the business fundamentals can prove more impactful than any advertising campaign, content marketing program or lead generation effort.

That's why this first section is entirely dedicated to the building blocks of a customer-centric business – branding, products, messaging, pricing and operations. With this strong foundation in place, your small business will be well positioned to embark on programs that engage the customers you already have and reach the ones you want.

Headfirst Camps: Smiles, Waves & Customer Engagement

Headfirst Summer Camps operates day camps in Washington DC, Maryland and Virginia, and they run camps for five Major League Baseball teams, including the Washington Nationals, New York Yankees, Boston Red Sox, Atlanta Braves and Chicago Cubs. While the company's camps provide summer fun for kids that is second to none, it is the customer experience that is truly noteworthy for parents.

This small business is committed to its customers (families) from top to bottom. The camp has a dedicated customer experience associate on the team, and the Headfirst customer commitment is evident in every interaction with every member of the camp team and in every facet of the business, no matter how small.

For example, take the camp drop-off and pickup process. Carpool line is one of the most annoying parts of the camp experience for parents – waiting in line with dozens of other often-frazzled parents in the summer heat, only to drop off a kid who's griping about sunscreen or pick up a tired child after an activity-packed day of swimming, sports and crafts. Yet Headfirst has mastered the process, making it as pleasant as possible for parents.

The camp positions counselors along the line to direct traffic, keep cars moving and answer questions. Every counselor smiles and waves at every parent and child every day. Whether in blazing heat or pouring rain, the counselors are there with a positive attitude that shines through. And it isn't a forced flick of the hand or begrudging smile – genuine care is evident as each counselor engages with the families, their customers. Smiles and waves – are they really that big a deal? Yes. Very much so.

Headfirst has not only inserted the customer perspective into the minutiae of a carpool line, but it also demonstrates its commitment to customers through its ongoing family communications, use of social media, regular requests for (and integration of) feedback, generous discounts, accommodating cancellation and change policies, ever-expanding offerings and camper special experiences, family programming beyond the camp day, and more.

The camp regularly receives positive feedback, enjoys year-over-year growth, and generates noteworthy community buzz, all of which underscore that their commitment to customers at all levels is an investment in marketing that works.

The Bottom Line

Operations aren't always sexy. But how a customer engages with your business is as important as how they receive a marketing message. So take the time to focus on building a customer-centric foundation before launching promotions that drive new traffic to your website or customers into your store. Your campaigns will be far more effective as you'll be prepared to engage customers and make sales.

CHAPTER 3

THE RULES OF CUSTOMER-CENTRIC MARKETING

If you take away nothing else from this book, I hope that this chapter is the one that sticks. There aren't many rules when it comes to marketing, and despite what any number of blog posts and consultants selling their special sauce will tell you, there is no top 10 list of marketing tactics that are guaranteed to grow your business.

Good customer-centric marketing is all about adapting best practices to work for your business and for your customers. But there are a few rules that guide a customer-centric business and absolutely impact your ability to sell. These foundational ideas sit beneath all of the recommendations in the chapters that follow.

Rule #1: Make it easy.

Make it easy for customers to understand your offering, make it easy for them to buy your offering and make it easy for them to stay connected to your business. If a customer can't quickly and easily understand what you sell, how much it costs and how to purchase, they will move on to another option that's easier.

Rule #2: Be responsive.

First, determine what level of responsiveness is reasonable for your business. While a five-minute response time for every email isn't realistic, in today's connected business environment, 12-24 hours isn't unreasonable and a quicker response is expected via social media.

If your response time is longer because of a busy period, time out of the office, or any other reason, manage expectations. Whether by Facebook post, email auto-reply, or a sign in the window, let customers know what's up. And if you don't often check your voicemail or log on to Twitter, don't offer those options as ways for customers to engage with you. That's a recipe for disaster.

Rule #3: Anticipate your customers' needs and meet them.

If you don't, expect that someone else will. Yes, this means selling and reminding customers to buy. But selling is not about the super cheesy knife guy going door to door and interrupting everyone's day. Sales means proactively recognizing a customer need and being there to fulfill it. And it also means keeping in touch so that customers remember your business when they need to make a purchase.

Rule #4: Pay attention to the details.

Grammar and spelling matter. After all, if you don't take the time to get the details right for yourself, what confidence will customers have in your commitment to taking care of the details for them?

Rule #5: Do what you say you will.

Period. Deliver on commitments. No BS, no fluff. Deliver the value you promise in your marketing materials, websites and sales sheets. And don't oversell your capabilities. This applies equally to the expertise you bring to the table as a consultant and the attributes a product delivers. A customer will buy a smaller set of awesome before a wide-reaching swath of mediocre (or empty promises) any day.

> **"**
>
> If a customer can't quickly and easily understand what you sell, how much it costs and how to purchase, they will move on to another option that's easier.

Rule #6: Be smart.

Always be learning (services), innovating (product) and staying fresh (retail). If you want to be fabulous for your customers, you have to first be fabulous for yourself. Attend continuing education workshops and industry tradeshows. Read up on your industry and your customers. Stay on top of trends and fads. Don't become obsolete because you were too busy working *in* your business to work *on* your business.

Rule #7: Consider would-be customers as "customers."

After all, the goal is for them to become customers. The experience a prospect has with your company should be as strong as when they actually become a customer. And vice versa – no bait and switch on attention to customers' needs once they're actually in the door.

Rule #8: Don't feel pressured to utilize any marketing tactics.

Just because you can doesn't mean you should. And just because something is seemingly cool and it seems like everyone's doing it, doesn't mean it makes sense for your business.

Pick the tactics that make the most sense for your business objectives and customers – stick to those.

Rule #9: Remember that you are not your customer.

While you might be in your own target market, you are only one buyer. When making plans and decisions, consider the majority of your customers, not only your own perspective.

Rule #10: Be awesome.

Whatever you sell, no matter what communications you send or engagement you create, be excellent. If you're going to do something, do it right. Give your customers a reason to care. It's hard to overlook straight-up awesomeness.

THE BOTTOM LINE

There's no one silver bullet that works for every small business. There's no such thing as a "must do." And without adapting others' great marketing ideas to your business and your customers, your campaigns won't resonate. The rules of customer-centric marketing apply across strategies, campaigns and communications. And they apply no matter your business type or number of years in operation. So keep these in mind as you continue through this book and plan your customer engagement. They set the stage for great customer connections and relationships.

When A Great Buying Experience Isn't Enough

I'll never forget the time when the owner of a boutique – a client from a couple of years' prior – sent me a text two weeks before Christmas asking, "Has retail really changed this much overnight?" The exchange that followed revealed that holiday sales were down, responsiveness to social media posts was flailing and the business owner was feeling generally unsettled about the future of the business.

This business has an incredible in-store experience and deep relationships with its customers during the sales process. While the store carries inventory and sells some products off-the-shelf, the bulk of its revenue comes from custom orders.

Customers that work with the boutique love it. Yes, "work with" not "buy from" – it's truly a relationship and an engaged purchasing experience. Customers love that the owner knows them by name and remembers details about their families. They love that when they walk in, there's always time for them and they're never rushed in making decisions. They love the quality of the products sold and service received. They love that the store thinks about their needs as shoppers – providing quarters for meters (all parking in the neighborhood is on-street or in a garage with meters), as well as candy, water, coffee and tea for a quick pick-me-up.

Yet, growth was flat and, no, retail hadn't changed overnight. Rather, the business had not kept up with changing times. This boutique is the sole local provider of specialty products. That used to be enough to drive foot traffic and sales, but as both product information and purchasing options became increasingly available online, the demand for a local purveyor had waned. At the same time, the owner had admittedly put some key things on the back burner due to lack of time and more pressing needs in other areas of the business.

Rule #1 Fail – Complicated Registry Process

The store offers a registry for customers who want to create wish lists, but as technology for this offering (and other online tools) evolved, the boutique hadn't kept up. As a result, it was regularly losing sales to other, larger stores that made the registry process easier – from registry set up and management to gift purchasing and delivery. The boutique, meanwhile, was leaving both registrants and gift givers frustrated by a complicated process – definitely not making it easy.

Rule #3 Fail – Sporadic Communications

With a 10-year business history, the boutique has a sizable customer database, email list and social media following. While they do a notably great job with one-on-one communications, with only 24 hours in the day and a small staff, its email and social media communications are infrequent and haphazard. As a result, the store isn't top of mind for a quick gift or add-on purchase – missing opportunities to meet ongoing customer needs.

Rule #9 Fail – Online Buying Experience Doesn't Match the In-Store Experience

While the in-store experience was fantastic, the online experience was equally noteworthy... for the wrong reasons. The boutique's website was complicated to navigate, and it was difficult to complete a purchase. Additionally, the products available online didn't match in-store inventory. Some that were listed on the website were actually out of stock or discontinued, and many top-selling items in-store didn't appear online at all. As the store owner herself admits, she's a touch-and-experience kind of person, so she always focused on the in-store opportunity to engage. As a result, she let the online experience falter, assuming all customers seek information and make buying decisions as she does.

Is every small business going to thrive at every aspect of operations and communications every single day? No, clearly not. It's not possible. But with a focus on the rules, managing changing sales environments and evolving customer needs is possible.

CHAPTER 4

A CUSTOMER-CENTRIC BRAND

Nearly all small businesses have a logo. Whether created by a professional branding firm, an online service or the aspiring graphic designer who lives next door, it's often a first stop on the small business start-up train. Many new business owners think that by slapping a logo on business cards, storefront signage and t-shirts, the business is "branded." But logos are little more than a pretty picture if there's no meaning behind them.

Customer-centric businesses know what those logos stand for. They consider not only the kind of company they want to be, but also what kind of company their customers want to buy from. Their brands stand for those key attributes – not just perfectly contrasting blues and yellows splashed over a sans serif font alongside a funky icon.

Customer-centric brands are genuine and honest. They understand their business personality and embrace it. Customer-centric brands don't feel forced or overly planned. And the brands that try to be something they're not fail to deliver on their brand promise to customers time and again. Customers feel it and move on.

It sounds idealistic, right? That you can connect with customers simply by being genuine? Not at all. Customers are attracted to authenticity. They want to know who you are as a business and what you offer. So be yourself!

> **"**
>
> You cannot be everything to everyone. Consider who you are as a company and the specific customers you want to serve.

Take the time to define your brand. Consider who you want to be as a company and what your target market expects. What attributes do you want customers to think of when they think about your business? Write them down. Live by them. Use these ideals as the backdrop for defining everything in your business – your products, your hiring practices, your retail environment, your marketing communications and your customer service approach. Everything.

Consistency is as key to creating an impactful brand as the brand's attributes themselves. Consistency allows your customers to know what to expect from you and empowers you to build on the overall brand experience with every interaction.

There's no right or wrong when it comes to your brand. It's your business – you get to set the tone and direction. As you think through your brand, however, keep in mind that both your brand and offerings do not need to be attractive to absolutely every potential buyer in the market. You cannot be everything to everyone. Consider who you are as a company and the specific customers you want to serve.

As you're defining your brand values, think through your ideal customer profile and their values as well. After all, how can a business be truly customer-centric without a deep understanding of its customers?

Get beyond your customer's demographic profile – the age, income bracket, geographic location, etc. – and consider what's important to both your typical customer and your ideal customer. If you've been in business awhile and are looking to address a different market or shift your delivery model, your current typical customer and your ideal future customer may not be the same. Outline your customers' values – what's important to them? Write these down, too.

> **"**
>
> Consider where the overlap between your focus and your customers' ideals occur. That's your sweet spot.

Now revisit your list. Check yourself. Are the customer values you outlined truly representative of their perspective or what you hope they care about? Be honest with yourself about what your customers think and value. If you're not sure, ask!

Take a peek at the two lists. Does your brand address a need your ideal customers seek or principle they hold dear? Are you trying to serve too wide an audience? Or are you limiting yourself to a particular niche? Consider where the overlap between your focus and your customers' ideals occur. That's your sweet spot.

With this in mind, you can apply your brand to your product or service offering, your pricing model, your customer service plan and your "marketing." We'll talk more about products, pricing and customer-centric communications in the chapters that follow.

Meghan Leahy Parent Coach:
Honesty, Candor & Tough Love

Meghan Leahy is a Washington DC-based parent coach. She works with parents to help them support their children through the tough stuff. Meghan's brand is one based on honesty and candor. Yes, she empowers and provides strategies. But Meghan tells it like it is – calling a spade a spade. She's unapologetic for her perspective and approach – one that is grounded in child development theory, brain science and love. Hers is a powerful combination that she's the first to admit isn't right for everyone.

Meghan's brand shines through in how she engages with clients in consultations and how she connects with a broader audience through content marketing. Through Facebook, Twitter, Instagram, her blog and her contributed column in *The Washington Post*, she's (sometimes) brutally honest. She shares stories of her own parenting struggles. She addresses tough topics like gun control and internet safety. And she talks about challenges faced by parents everywhere – power struggles with their kids, sibling rivalry, handling holidays and extended family, and just getting through the day-to-day of meals, dressing, sleeping and bathing.

When working with clients, she pushes them hard. She calls clients out when they're projecting their own bias onto their kids and challenges this with tough love. As a result, people connect with Meghan's brand. In just five years, she amassed a Facebook following of nearly 8,500 (as of May 2016), is booked out weeks in advance (though she's always there for clients in crisis) and is a sought-after speaker on myriad parenting topics. Why? She's real. Her brand connects with customers.

Something else to keep in mind: In many cases, your customer will not be the end user of your product or beneficiary of your service. Consider the mom who buys batting lessons for her budding baseball star. Think about the single man buying a wedding gift for a coworker.

And if you sell a product, you very likely may have multiple "customers." Remember that your distribution partners – the retailers or others who carry your product and resell it to a wider audience – are customers, too. Be sure to create customer profiles for these channel partners and consider their buying habits and needs as you outline your campaigns.

"

Consistency is as key to creating an impactful brand as the brand's attributes themselves. Consistency allows your customers to know what to expect from you and empowers you to build on the overall brand experience with every interaction.

The Bottom Line

Your brand is far more than your logo, color palette and fonts. Your brand is everything you stand for as a business – your values, your ideals, your guiding principles. And while your brand won't resonate with every potential customer in the market, it should guide your business in engaging with those truly in your target market. A customer-centric brand also has a clear understanding of its customers' values, ideals and guiding principles, as these set the foundation for creating an emotional connection with them. With your business brand and your customer profile clearly defined...

- Revisit your brand and customer outlines. Are they aspirational or truly who you are as a business and your customers are as buyers? Being genuine is a must and that starts with being honest with yourself.

- Embrace your brand in all you do. Consistency is key for customers to know what to expect and be able to easily connect with your business.

- Remember your customers may include more than just the end user of your product or service. As you move through the ideas outlined in the chapters that follow, consider every layer of customer in your sales channel and develop campaigns for each. While every customer needs engagement and outreach, not every customer type connects in the same way.

Chapter 5

Defining What You Sell

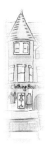

An honest brand that permeates your small business lies at the heart of your company. But clearly defined products and services are equally important – they're the core of your offering. (In chapters 7 and 8, we'll get to pricing and operations – the last critical pieces that make up the foundation of your business' profitability.)

When it comes to defining what you sell, oftentimes less is more. With a menu of too many choices, customers' eyes glaze over and struggle to settle on anything. This is not to say that you can't offer a large inventory of choices – in many cases, particularly for retailers, it's sometimes the nature of the business.

In many cases, however, small business owners tend to increase their list of offerings and capabilities in an effort to please new audiences and bring in new business. While seemingly a positive on the surface, in reality, too many offerings confuses customers (which stands in their way of buying) and poses a challenge (at best) for companies that want to execute well.

Remember you aren't for everyone and that's ok. Go back to your brand that you already defined and are committed to. Recognize that you have limitations – that, too, is ok. In fact, it's better than ok. It's great. By specializing, you can be an excellent choice for your ideal customers rather than a mediocre choice for the masses. In the last chapter, we discussed your ideal customer; there's a subset of the many, many offerings you could deliver that is likely most appropriate for them.

Whether you're a service provider that delivers only two offerings or a retailer with thousands of SKUs, find a niche. Your niche might be broad like mine – all small businesses – or super narrow like the speech coach who works only with female attorneys looking to change careers in the Washington DC area. In defining your niche, recognize both your own limitations and future opportunities. Start by focusing on a niche that you can do a really great job at supporting today. And then be open to expansion and growth to new target markets over time so you can both grow your small business and share your talents and offerings with more and more customers.

Do you have room to trim your offerings? Or perhaps you need to add to the list? As you evaluate your products and services, ask yourself a few key questions:

- How many offerings do you have?

- Are all of your offerings profitable?

- Which offerings do you like selling/executing the most?

- Which offerings are you best at?

- Which offerings align with your core values and capabilities?

Just because you can offer a service or stock a product doesn't mean you should. Perhaps you simply don't like delivering on the offering. Or maybe you're hoping to take your business in a different direction. This is absolutely ok.

On the flip side, while an offering might not be super profitable, it might make sense to keep it around. Do you break even on it or make a small profit? Does it draw in other, more profitable business? Does it provide great value to existing customers?

Your answers to all of these questions will help you decide on today's list of offerings. I say today's, because nothing is set in stone. Ever. You're the driver of your business and because you're small, you have all the flexibility in the world to make a change. You can phase out something old or phase in something new over time. Just be careful not to change course too frequently, as you'll confuse your customers (and likely your team, too).

When You Have Many Offerings

Retail stores and restaurants often have a large list of offerings. If you fall in these categories, your job is to ease the purchasing decision for your customers. Explore ways to group choices by category to help a customer work their way through the options.

Iron Rooster, a restaurant in Annapolis, MD, does a great job with this. The menus, which vary by time of day, are pages long and offer choices ranging from an assortment of benedicts and sandwiches at brunch to all-day breakfast to a host of burger choices alongside other sandwiches and main courses at dinner. Yet they're each well organized and easy to navigate. (Making a decision on what to order from among the many awesome options, however, is another story. My recommendation is to go with friends and share.)

The notion of categorizing offerings applies equally to service providers. Consider grouping your capabilities so a client easily understands your service offerings and can determine if they're relevant for them.

Special Requests

An important note: You may offer, or have the ability to offer, services and special order products beyond those that you list on your website and display in your store. The recommendations in this chapter do not mean you can't choose to deliver on special requests. The customers who already know you will know to ask. And those who aren't sure are typically bold enough to ask as well. With more clearly defined offerings, you can choose whether to deliver on these special requests or not.

Consider our favorite local brick oven pizza place that changed its menu three years before I wrote this book. In doing so, the restaurant took off my favorite veggie pizza. The fact is, I was one of only a small group that loved their combination of sweet potato, asparagus, broccoli, red onion, roasted tomatoes and smoked gouda. Seriously, it was amazing. The "arrabiata" was replaced on the menu with a more traditional veggie pizza option. But when we're there, if the chef has the ingredients in the kitchen, she's happy to make it for me. I ask, and the restaurant delivers. Everyone's happy.

Special requests happen all the time for service providers, too. If you're a service provider capable of and interested in delivering on the customer request, by all means, go for it! Or, if not, refer it to another, more appropriate service provider. Either way, the buying decision was made easier for the customer.

THE BOTTOM LINE

You can always offer more products and services. But really hone in on what you want to be selling. Narrow your offerings to those your customers want to buy. Identify those that are most profitable. Specializing allows you to be excellent at a niche rather than so-so at a broad range of areas.

There are, of course, special circumstances. That's absolutely ok.

- When More Makes Sense: In cases where a longer list of offerings is appropriate, guide your customers toward a decision that's right for them by categorizing the choices.

- Special Requests: Customers will always ask for capabilities beyond those you promote. When you're specific up front, you can choose to meet the request or not depending on the situation.

By focusing on where your strengths meet your customers' desires, you make it easier for your customers to buy and you position yourself to deliver in the best way possible.

CHAPTER 6

TALKING ABOUT WHAT YOU SELL

With all due respect to the many talented copywriters out there, sometimes we need to skip the marketing speak. We need to skip the jargon and buzzwords. Just tell would-be customers what you do! If you can't explain it, they can't buy it. If you can't explain it, the value isn't clear. If you can't explain it, you can't deliver on your promise. Rule #1– make it easy. If a customer can't quickly and easily understand what you sell, they simply can't buy – and they won't stick around long enough to figure it out.

> " If you can't explain it, they can't buy it. If you can't explain it, the value isn't clear. If you can't explain it, you can't deliver on your promise.

According to Forrester Research, 55 percent of U.S. adults online are likely to abandon their purchase if they can't find a quick answer to their question.[1] That means that more than half of your customers could walk away simply because your website is too confusing or information is too hard to find. Yikes.

As small business owners, we often focus too much on value and forget the "what." We're almost too intent on justifying why our approach, differentiator or special sauce is worth it. Yes – you do need to clarify your value proposition. Absolutely. But you also need to clearly and plainly say what you do. Consider these one-liners (yes, they're real):

Description: "I serve as a trusted business advisor."
Translation: I'm a small business attorney.
Challenge: This man is often confused for a business consultant, CPA or coach rather than the lawyer he is. While his bio references his Juris Doctorate and his listing of services include litigation and contracts, it never once references that he is a small business attorney.

Description: "We deliver digital solutions."
Translation: We build websites and mobile apps.
Challenge: While some website visitors understand that this company does more than just churn out generic WordPress websites, for many of this company's prospective small business clients, the term "digital solutions" feels out of reach for their needs and budget. . . which couldn't be further from the case.

Description: "I'm a life stylist."
Translation: I'm a professional organizer, personal stylist, and event planner.

Challenge: Life stylist perfectly captures how this small business owner impacts her clients' entire lives – including physical space, mental clutter, personal habits, and daily activities. However, prospective customers can't easily identify with this new term. Additionally, while the benefits she offers touch all aspects of your life, prospective customers are often looking for solutions in only one area.

A quick and easy understanding of your offering – whether product or service – empowers customers to recognize and embrace what you offer and move further down the path toward a sale. It doesn't matter if you introduce yourself and the business to potential customers at a networking event or tradeshow, in your retail environment, on your website, on Amazon or in your print materials. Keep it simple.

A simple explanation also makes it really easy for others to refer potential business to you. While a friend, family member or someone else in your network may not be a prospect, if they have a clear understanding of what you offer, they have the ability to identify opportunities, introduce your offerings and recommend that others contact you.

BETTER ELEVATOR PITCHES

Using clear language when discussing what you sell is essential for your elevator pitch. Here's my formula for any introduction:

1. A simple statement about what you do. No buzzwords. No value proposition fluff. Just who you are – plain and simple.
   The Outcome: The listener "gets" what you offer.

2. Who you help. Define what "clients" or "customers" means to you. (More on the importance of this below.) *The Outcome:* The listener sees themselves or someone else they know as a good fit for your offering.

3. Quick examples of how your ideal customers benefit from your product or service. *The Outcome:* The listener understands how your offering benefits them or someone else they know.

There's only one goal for an elevator pitch – to be asked a question in return. You want the listener (a potential customer, partner, distributor, or referral source) to be intrigued enough to want to know more so the conversation continues. In that conversation, you'll have the ability to get in all those extra details you're dying to share, like what differentiates you from the competition and the value you provide (aka, why you're worth the investment).

So what's your elevator pitch?

> "
> There's only one goal for an elevator pitch – to be asked a question in return.

If you're feeling stuck, write down everything you'd normally include in your pitch. Then, strip out the adjectives. Once you have the core of the message down, add back in only the descriptor words that truly enhance and clarify your pitch rather than clutter the message.

With an elevator pitch you feel great about, practice! Ask your mom, a friend, a colleague or an accountability partner to listen to you. Once you feel confident delivering your message, move on to your existing customers or those in your target market. While friends can provide feedback on your tone of voice and general clarity of message, if they're not your target customer, the value of their feedback is limited to their perspective and likely not representative of your customer's. Make sure what you think you're saying is really what your customer is hearing.

You can use this same construction of ideas as a launching point to outline the rest of your talking points, too. This same model applies to how you talk about your services or products.

On "Clients" and "Customers"

A quick note on the term "clients" and "customers." No matter what you call the folks who buy from your business, too often, those words creep into our elevator pitches and other materials without any further clarification. Who are these people? Men or women? New moms or retirees? The elite athlete or weekend warrior? Be sure to describe your ideal customer so that would-be buyers can easily see themselves as the perfect fit for your products or services.

After The Introduction:
Websites, Print Materials, & Content Marketing

Another common pitfall of small business communications is the overwhelming compulsion to say absolutely everything in every message. You don't have to! And you really shouldn't.

Rather, all of your communications should work together to provide a complete picture of your business. Customers are busy. They don't have time or interest to read extensive, loquacious copy on each and every page of your website. So respect your customer's time enough to balance being direct and to the point with the desire and need to add words to your webpages to answer likely questions and support SEO.

On the flip side, don't forget that you're the expert in your business and your industry. What's obvious to you might not be as evident or top of mind for a prospective customer. There are times when educating is essential, and there are nuances and details you need to provide to help customers make a purchasing decision. Remember to provide any necessary context so your message is clear. Also, take advantage of opportunities and places where customers look for additional information – FAQ pages on websites, detailed brochures, or links to more information. The key is to make sure that the details don't get in the way of the basics.

When it comes to going deeper and providing more information, be sure to not only provide the answers, but also the questions, too. Sometimes prospective customers don't know what they don't know. Help them to understand the key points and details they need to make a smart purchasing decision – whether from you or a competitor. Educate and inform. The understanding of a concept or product category goes a long way toward making you the authority in a customer's mind – and more likely to win the sale.

You also want to address objections head on in your communications. In doing so, you may lose a customer or two. But the clarity you afford to customers far outweighs the loss of those not in your sweet spot. And there will be times when you will have to justify yourself. Oftentimes when this occurs, it will be in public over social media. There's more on responding to criticism in chapter 13.

Last, but certainly not least, don't forget to sell yourself! Beyond your value-added content marketing (more on this in future chapters, too), tell a prospective customer what to do next. Include a call to action, like "Buy Now!" buttons. Don't ask – tell people. Instead of saying "If you're interested in learning more…" say "To learn more…."

That is far more powerful. Assume your prospect wants more information. Don't be afraid to be confident. You've built an awesome business, invented a life-changing product, or deliver a valuable service – be proud and excited to share it with others.

Beyond Words – Your Physical Environment

Appearance is everything. For small businesses with a retail store, office space or any other bricks and mortar location, the physical environment can speak louder than words. And what the space says must match your words in both clarity and consistency of message and brand. The physical space can sometimes be your customer's first impression of your business – setting the stage for their reaction to your offering. And for repeat customers, it reinforces their understanding of your brand, your business and your offering.

For example, I often think of the vice principal I met at a customer service training program. We talked about the importance of the school environment. While not often thought of as a "business," private schools are very much a business operation, and the vice principal attended the training because quality service lies at the heart of both her school's student programming and family engagement. The school works tirelessly to keep the school clean and organized. And it has invested in interior design and windows that make it bright and full of natural light. These physical touches directly contribute to both prospective families' impressions of the school and – importantly – students' ability to engage and to learn. By investing in the tangible communication of its brand, the school has increased enrollment (revenue) and student performance (engagement).

THE BOTTOM LINE

Always communicate succinctly and clearly. The goal of each communication is to move a prospective customer further down the sales pipeline or directly to a sale. When you are direct and focused in your introductions and communications, customers can more easily understand your offering and make a purchasing decision. Clear communications also empower others to more easily refer others to you.

So reread your website, your brochures and even your new business proposals. Consider how you introduce yourself at networking events. Look at your physical space. Be really honest with yourself – if you didn't know your business, would you understand it clearly enough in 30 seconds or less to want to learn more, much less buy from you? If not, take a step back and clearly outline what you offer, who you serve and how your customers benefit from your product or service.

Of course there is often a need for greater detail. But with a clear introduction, customers will continue the conversation and pursue the additional information rather than be turned off by up-front confusion.

CHAPTER 7

CUSTOMER-CENTRIC PRICING & DISCOUNTS

There are tons of books, models and theories on pricing. Your pricing model may offer three packages with the goal of urging customers to opt for the mid-priced choice. Or perhaps you sell everything a la carte, or you only offer products or services that are customized specifically for each client. Any of these models can work and I'll leave pricing theory to the financial folks. In this chapter, we'll look at pricing from your customer's point of view.

Once you've determined the general pricing structure that supports your revenue and profitability goals, layer in your customers. Ensure that regardless of the model you choose, you charge an amount that's fair and appropriate for both you and your customer. Pricing should reflect your experience in the field, quality of materials or ingredients used, value you deliver, competitor availability and pricing, and price sensitivity of your customers.

If you choose to create packages, then combine products or services with appropriate value-added benefits or additions so the offering is both comprehensive and clear as to what is included. Refer to rule #1 again: make it easy to buy from your business by making it easy to understand how much something costs and then making it easy to complete the purchase. Your customer shouldn't have to work to determine how much your product or service costs! A caveat – this isn't to say that all of your pricing needs to appear on your website or be publicly displayed. But it is important to give prospective customers an idea of how much they can expect to spend to work with your business – no matter how large or small the amount.

While you might have the best product on the market, if buying is difficult or complicated, you'll lose sales and frustrate customers. So, price and package your offerings according to the product you sell and the customer you're targeting. While a seemingly obvious takeaway, it isn't always so. By way of example, I offer my own experience with the quest for a personalized baby blanket.

As you know by now, I am a lover of all things small business. Shopping small (and local when I can) is always my preference when it comes to gift giving. I love supporting the mom-and-pop around the corner and sharing the amazing products with friends and family who otherwise wouldn't have a way to be introduced to them. (More on the power of word of mouth in chapter 12.) So when a friend had twins a few years back, I first turned to the website of a local, home-based business from which I had received a number of adorable, high quality baby gifts for my own boys.

While the personalized baby blanket options were perfect, I was completely confused as to the total cost. For one blanket style, the first line of personalization was included, but each additional word was extra. For another, every line of embroidered text was a separate charge. Since I wanted to buy two blankets – one for each of the twins – the math quickly got complicated. Much as I loved this business, I moved on to another. And then another. What I discovered was that in the world of baby gifts, "personalized baby blanket" rarely equals personalization included. The result? I went big and bought from Pottery Barn Kids. Why? It was easy.

I completely understand that additional lines of embroidery equal more thread and more time to sew, driving up the cost of goods sold. But if just one of those small businesses I tried to patronize had clear pricing, they would have quickly made the sale. And more than that, they could have easily gained a customer who would return to buy more when the inevitable next gift is needed.

"

While you might have the best product on the market, if buying is difficult or complicated, you'll lose sales and frustrate customers.

A Few Notes on Fees

In the last example, I'm guessing (hoping) that the small businesses I tried to patronize were well intentioned and attempting to give customers the option to buy something at a lower cost by breaking out the add-on costs. However, in the case of personalization, the add-ons are part of the product itself, which leads me to the next key to customer-friendly pricing and operations. Grab your seat belt, I know I ruffle a lot of feathers with this recommendation.

Your business expenses do not equal your customers' costs. So being customer-centric means that you cannot charge extra for payments made via credit card, a fee for parking in your parking lot or for the time spent traveling to a customer's location. I know, I know. I can hear you grumbling and rolling your eyes, "But it costs me money for customers to pay with a credit card!" Yup, sure does. But if you choose to offer customers the option to pay with a credit card or state that you service a defined territory, it shouldn't cost your customers extra to take advantage of the operating model you set forth. It just feels icky (yes, that's the official business term). The goal is customer love – not customer ugh.

Credit Cards

If you choose to accept credit cards, this is an operational decision. Yes, it's true that while you don't have to accept credit cards, in today's often buy-now-pay-later economy, it is expected. I'm a fan of offering a credit card (or PayPal) option, as it is more customer friendly (you're giving them a choice) and better for your bottom line (you'll get paid more quickly). While some businesses offer a discount for payment by cash or check to encourage this desired behavior, it complicates the decision making process for the customer. And it inherently passes the cost along in a different way.

Absorb the fees and take the associated tax deduction. (The fees you pay to credit card processors are business expenses – talk to your accountant about the specifics of your situation.) Customer-centric pricing = one price, regardless of payment method.

Parking Fees

If you're like many small businesses, you don't own your building. In some cases, you may have to rent your parking lot, too (if you're lucky enough to have one in a trendy urban setting!). If parking is essentially necessary to patronize your retail store or office, do not charge your customers to park. If you operate out of a building with third-party operated parking, validate parking for customers (if possible and permissible with the parking lot owner/operator). The goal is for the customer experience to be seamless and without unexpected costs.

I'll use my own experience as an example again. A couple of years ago, we went whale watching off the coast of Cape Cod. We selected from the different boat operators based on proximity to where we were staying, price, and importantly, reviews from previous passengers. I made reservations online and paid for what I was led to believe were all-inclusive tickets. The excursion wasn't inexpensive, but it felt worth it for the once-in-a-lifetime experience.

Upon arrival at the boathouse, however, we were greeted with a $25 parking fee. First impression – ick. But there was no other option – we were at the end of a tiny, narrow road with nothing but the tour company's boathouse in sight. While the whales were breathtaking and the naturalist on board entertaining, I always mention the parking fee when recommending this tour operator.

For small businesses that have to rent a parking area separate from their existing space, the costs can be steep. But rather than pass them through to customers as separate line items, factor them into your overall cost and consider them when determining your pricing. That way, your pricing will be truly all-inclusive, customer friendly and easy to understand.

Travel Fees

For professional service providers who work both on-site at a customer's location and in your own office or studio, travel fees can seem reasonable when the distance exceeds the desired or core service area. However, this is another area that can quickly make customers feel nickel-and-dimed, which leads to the ick factor.

Rather than charging customers a nominal fee that likely doesn't cover the cost of gas or extra travel time at your billable rate, limit your service area and refer those outside the area to another professional. Alternatively, you can charge a set price for in-studio/office appointments and another higher amount for those that are on-site at the customer's location, regardless of location. If you choose to service a wider, but still relatively local area, this is your choice as the business owner and not a choice that should become a customer cost.

Service area radius and associated travel fees fall into the same bucket as limiting service offerings. Clearly define the area you service, and make it easy for a customer to determine if they are a good fit for you based on those parameters. Prospective customers outside of your geographic area will still ask about working with you, and you can choose whether to say yes or no.

A final note on travel fees and caveat on the recommendations above. For business requests well outside of your stated geographic area, travel fees are appropriate and reasonable. In determining your travel fee, however, consider reasonable costs – mileage, if driving, or airfare. Some small business owners factor in billable hours for travel time, though I'm a fan of using this time for other billable work or personal time (otherwise the travel fee could be cost prohibitive, and you could lose the sale).

What's "reasonable" will depend on your customer. Large businesses or highly affluent individual customers likely can afford and are accustomed to higher reimbursable expenses, while small businesses or individual customers are typically far more price sensitive.

On Couponing and Discounts

Coupons and sales are terrific for introducing new products and highlighting specific offerings, for rewarding new and existing customers and for driving sales during otherwise slow periods. But keep in mind as you're planning your promotions that the goal for discounts is to drive sales.

First, make sure the specials are truly that – special. If everything is always on sale, customers will question the value of your products and have little incentive to pay full price. This isn't to say you can't offer a special or discount every month – just make sure that each deal is unique and will help you achieve one of the goals noted above.

Second, ensure your coupons are easy to use. Don't offer $2 off of a purchase over $10 when all of the items for which the coupon applies cost $9.49. The goal is to encourage a purchase, not force a customer to buy more than they need.

Last, give your customers the deal. If a customer is ready to make a purchase, but realizes at the register that they've forgotten their coupon, give them the discount anyway. Or perhaps a customer tries to use a coupon or apply a service discount two days after it expired. Again, make good on the offer. Remember, you offered the deal to encourage purchase, not to frustrate customers. By being a stickler for the details, you'll likely lose the sale altogether and have a cranky customer who tells others. Making good on the offer (even with a gentle reminder of the details) will win customer hearts and wallets.

This is not to say to give everything away for steal. The goal is always sales. Incentivizing customers to buy is just one way to get there. When offers are planned and executed with business goals and customer buying habits in mind, everyone wins – your small business can win the sale and customers can enjoy your product or service at a discount.

The Bottom Line

The key to customer-centric pricing is simplicity. Make your pricing easy to understand and the details on what's included clear. And don't add on extra fees – the nominal revenue they bring in leave customers feeling nickel-and-dimed. When it comes to putting your offering on sale, make the deals clear and honor discounts you offer. With all pricing and discounting, the goal is sales – plain and simple.

Chapter 8

Running A Customer-Centric Operation

On the surface, it might seem that operations, like pricing, must compromise business profitability and efficiency if they're to become customer–centric. However, this couldn't be further from the truth. Running a customer-centric business doesn't mean you cannot have standard operating procedures or terms and conditions. It also doesn't mean that you must bend the rules and customize your policies for each customer's needs. It doesn't mean you have to say yes to every ask.

Rather, running a customer-centric operation is about getting back to basics: delivering excellence in the offerings you choose to sell. Being customer-centric is about making your policies reasonable and attractive for a customer so that they want to do business with you. It's about providing customers with an understanding of how and why you operate the way you do. And it's about delivering excellent customer service – top to bottom. There's no one chapter in this book dedicated to customer service. Customer service isn't a function or a job description. Delivering excellence throughout the entire customer lifecycle – through every sale, every communication and every engagement – that's customer service.

Policies & Procedures

In a customer-centric business, policies and procedures can position your small business to better serve your customers and help your customers better engage with you. Policies can serve as a guide to help you hire the best resources, produce the best product or pass savings along to customers.

While customers may not always like your policies, when you clearly and politely explain the "why" behind them, they are far more accepting of them. Having them in place provides customers structure and parameters for working with your business. And that's customer centric.

The old adage, "the customer is always right" is flawed. Sometimes they're wrong. Sometimes they're unreasonable. Sometimes they're downright nasty. But they still expect and deserve service with a smile. Take the high road, because your customer-centric approach and customer-friendly policies position you to work through the tough situations. Established policies empower you to stand your ground when necessary and make concessions when appropriate. An understanding approach enables your customers to feel heard and supported even when they don't deserve your kindness, which is unfortunately sometimes the reality.

Back to the positive... Remember my quest to buy monogrammed baby blankets? I have another baby gifting story, but this one lands in the plus column.

When my niece was born, I wanted to send cupcakes to my sister in the hospital. A quick Facebook query to friends reminded me yet again of the power of word of mouth. My Facebook friends pointed me to a popular local bakery in Boston, where my sister lives. When I placed my order and requested same-day delivery, I was told no. The bakery makes only one delivery run each day to the hospitals in the area – it's the only way this small business can accommodate multiple delivery locations with a small team (the majority of the store's business was in-store). I had missed that day's window.

This might sound like it was turning into a negative experience – quite the contrary. The bakery clearly and pleasantly explained the rationale of its policy, and they made the purchasing experience a breeze – I didn't even need to know the hospital's address or my sister's room number. The bakery made the gift-giving process seamless. They delivered delicious and freshly made cupcakes in beautiful packaging the next day as promised. My sister loved them.

> **"**
> The old adage, "the customer is always right" is flawed. Sometimes they're wrong. Sometimes they're unreasonable. Sometimes they're downright nasty. But they still expect and deserve service with a smile.

Or consider another small business, Golden Girls Network, an online roommate matching service for baby boomer women. The company works in the same way as an online dating website – members create profiles outlining their attributes and their preferences, and then they search for an ideal match.

Sometimes the business owner receives complaints that non-members are unable to view member details without creating a member profile themselves. This is intentional, as it helps protect the privacy of the members while fostering an environment of mutual trust. As a result, the business owner will not budge on this policy. To participate in the community and use the website's functionality, membership and a minimum profile are required. This operating model is clearly and politely explained to anyone who questions it, an approach that provides peace of mind to members and fosters their confidence that Golden Girls Network values them as customers.

Every Minute Counts

We've already talked about the busy lives of today's customers. A customer-centric operation recognizes the value of a customer's time and how much of their time they're committing to engage with the business. How often have you been at your doctor's office and felt frustrated that you have to write the same personal details – name, address, date of birth, phone numbers, email address – at the top of each and every form? While the forms may serve different purposes or be used by different departments, a small business that's customer-centric will find ways to streamline the forms.

Customer-centric businesses also demonstrate that they value their customers' time by both keeping appointments and being on time for meetings. While emergencies occur and schedule changes are sometimes unavoidable – especially for the busy entrepreneur wearing many, many hats – being reliable is a sign of customer respect. Small businesses that respect their customers earn respect in return. Yes, this is possible even for doctors' offices, most of which are small businesses themselves.

The Geller Law Group:
Professionalism Meets Playdates

Attorney Rebecca Geller is upfront about the fact that she started her law firm, The Geller Law Group, to create a business that worked for her lifestyle.

As a mom of three kids, Rebecca wanted the ability to do great work for her small business, nonprofit and family clients without sacrificing quality time with her young family – an occupational hazard for many female attorneys. Rebecca also wanted to offer her clients a big firm experience with a small firm feeling and rates.

Offering high-caliber attorneys who do quality work is about where the "big firm" similarities stop. The Geller Law Group doesn't boast leather- and mahogany-clad offices or a staff that dons matching black suits and wingtips. In fact, they don't have a traditional office at all. The team co-works in a shared office environment, or they work from home. Sometimes their laptops are with them on the pool deck during swim team practice or their iPads are used to answer quick inquiries while waiting in the carpool line (with the car in park, of course). Rebecca is quick to note, "This doesn't mean that kids are in the office. There's work time and mom time." Sometimes her team sneaks work in between mom commitments, but they don't blur the line between the two.

The firm's approach is centered on what works for the firm's employees – family comes first – but the approach also resonates with its clients. "Our clients feel that they know us and they identify with us, especially women." Rebecca says. "They say, 'I want to support your firm, because I support women-owned businesses and I support the way you run your business.'"

The Geller Law Group holds steadfast to its family-first policies. When a prospective client requests a meeting at night or on the weekend, they're told no. Rebecca points out that "this isn't how we work. While we might work off-hours, we won't commit to being available at those times." The firm has never lost a client because of this. But the firm also recognizes that sometimes, there are situations that demand immediate attention, and they always address truly urgent situations immediately. Rebecca points out that the team is adept at separating the real emergencies from those that clients consider "emergencies."

Making family a priority does not mean that The Geller Law Group sacrifices quality, however. Their clients expect and appreciate the firm's passion for delivering excellent work in a timely manner. The firm commits to responding to all inquiries and needs within 24 hours, but not two hours – or two minutes. And they make good on this promise, with work always done on time and with consistent quality – regardless of whether it is completed at 2pm or midnight.

The commitment to its brand and transparency with clients, coupled with its focus on excellence, has proven incredibly successful for The Geller Law Group. In 2016, less than five years after opening its "doors," the firm hired its tenth employee and averaged eight new clients every week. It surpassed the 1,500-client mark and practiced in five states. And because of her approach, Rebecca has unintentionally become a national thought leader on work-life balance and women at work.

The Bottom Line

Achieving customer-centric operational efficiency may seem like an idealistic dream. Small businesses face numerous day-to-day operating demands and sometimes it feels like enough just to keep the lights on and the ship running. However, it is possible. Like everything else in a customer-centric business, you are going beyond simply delivering a great product to considering your customer's needs and perspectives.

Policies provide your customers with a framework and a set of expectations for working with your business, and they empower you to stand firm on your approach or make a customer feel loved by making concessions.

Time. There's never enough. But when you respect your customers' time, you demonstrate how much you value their schedules and the moments they choose to share with your business. And you not only give customers a few minutes back in their day, but you reap the benefit of a more organized schedule – increasing productivity and gaining a few precious moments back in your day, too.

Section 2

CUSTOMER-CENTRIC COMMUNICATIONS & ENGAGEMENT

Chapter 9

Make New Friends, But Keep The Old

"Make new friends, but keep the old."

When I was a little girl and a proud member of Girl Scout Troop 106 of the Girl Scout Council of the Nation's Capital, this concept was ingrained in us through activities and song. (Yes, Scouting alums, I can hear you singing at home.) And the premise is taught well beyond Girl Scouts to all children as they come back to school each fall from summer break thrilled to see friends from the previous year, but encouraged to welcome new students into their classrooms.

Yet somehow, what's ingrained in us as children is often lost in adulthood. As small business owners, we're so focused on growth and what's next that we sometimes forget to nurture what we already have. But why? Generating sales by engaging existing customers is both more likely and less expensive than selling to new customers. According to the research firm Market Metrics, the probability of selling to a new prospect is 5 to 20 percent while the probability of selling to an existing customer is 60 to 70 percent.[2] Couple that with the stat from Forrester Research that shows that acquiring new customers can cost five time more than satisfying and retaining current customers.[3] Wow.

These numbers are anecdotally reinforced by small business owners every day. Look at your numbers. Do the majority of sales come from existing customers? Most likely, they do. This notion of marketing to your existing customers applies even to highly transactional service businesses, such as mortgage brokers, wedding planners and realtors, considering their high rate of referral business. Referrals lie at the heart of new business from existing customers.

So before you dive into the shiny new marketing programs that "guarantee" thousands of new customers, start by engaging your existing customers. Connect with them. Deepen your relationship with them. Reward them. Customer engagement encompasses each and every way your business connects with a customer throughout their lifecycle. It is the foundation of customer relationships.

The impact of, as well as the opportunity and need for, strong (and better) customer engagement is real. According to a survey of more than 6,000 customers on expectations for local businesses, "offers for returning customers" was cited as the best way for a local business to stand out from the competition. The research went on to note that a big gap exists between the variety and frequency of different types of communication, such as service/appointment reminders and advice/helpful tips they currently receive from local businesses and what they are open to receiving.[4] The takeaway? You're most certainly not being pushy or annoying by connecting more frequently or engaging more deeply. Customers want small businesses to make the effort and show them love.

Beyond the desire for greater engagement, customers also expect more from small businesses – expectations they're willing to pay for. The same research on local business customers found that not only do 96% of consumers think small, local businesses offer more personalized service than large, national chains, but 72% are also willing to pay more for better quality from a local establishment.[5]

The numbers are strong. The business benefits of customer engagement are noteworthy. Still need convincing? Let's talk emotion. How annoying is it to see deep discounts advertised only to find "new customers only" hidden in the fine print? Or to make a purchase only to experience a rate hike or substantial decline in service after a few months? Where's the customer focus in that?

Customer engagement is about creating customer love. It's about going beyond customer satisfaction to build true customer relationships.

Customers who already know you and buy from you have different information needs than those unfamiliar with your offerings. The offers that resonate to drive sales vary depending on a customer's place in their relationship with your business and your products or services. And the communications, events and programs that resonate with existing customers versus new ones differ, too.

"

Customer engagement encompasses each and every way your business connects with a customer throughout their lifecycle. It is the foundation of customer relationships.

So, as you plan for your marketing programs, consider the audience for each effort. If your campaign is focused on engaging your existing customers, tailor your message and outreach to them. Just as your business can't be everything to everyone, neither can your marketing. Consider the audience and the goals for your marketing and adjust accordingly. It's tough to adequately support the needs of both existing and new customers – and your business goals – in a single communication or program.

The online stationery and personalized products company, Erin Condren Designs, rocks at customer engagement – and their strategy has evolved over the years as the company and its product set has grown. Years ago, the company sent out a bonus set of personalized labels with every order of labels. I'm still using mine up as I'm quite the label lover, and, as a loyal EC customer, I received several sets. While they no longer send out free customized product, orders still arrive beautifully packaged and, at least in the months as I was writing this book, with a bonus inspiration card or sticker included.

"

Customer engagement is about creating customer love. It's about going beyond customer satisfaction to build true customer relationships.

Beyond the giveaways, the company sends out coupons for existing customers only and special offers for those who haven't purchased in a while. As the company has grown, they've had a few missteps, as most small businesses do on their path to greatness. When customer service has faltered, social media has struck the wrong chord, or shipping has been slow, the company has accepted responsibility, issued apologies and made things right. Great engagement creates loyal customers.

The Bottom Line

Research proves and anecdotal evidence suggests that the bulk of your new business comes from your existing business. So instead of focusing your marketing dollars only on social media ads to garner new likes or deals only for new customers, first focus your marketing on those existing customers who provided you the funds to market in the first place.

Chapter 10

Getting Beyond The Monthly Newsletter: Great Communications

Most small businesses fall in one of two camps – either under-communicating for fear of annoying customers or over-communicating for fear of being forgotten. Neither is ideal.

Consider two boutique fitness studios, both of which have fabulous offerings, loyal customers and classes that are on trend. Neither has a membership model. Instead, both studios sell class packages and allow customers to sign up for spots in specific classes – but only for the coming week (a common practice in boutique fitness). Both studios have experienced a decrease in email open rates and a plateau in class registrations in the face of a substantial increase in competition.

- Studio 1 sends a monthly newsletter to its customers – including both regulars and those who have dropped in for only a class or two. The newsletter is notably long and requires readers to click "more" if they want to continue reading anything. While the content is good, it is almost entirely focused on the studio itself, including offers, new classes and special events. Despite the fact that class registrations pick up in the 24 hours immediately following the monthly email, Studio 1 has not increased the frequency of its emails, convinced customers would be annoyed by an increase in volume (though they never actually asked for feedback).

• Studio 2 sends two emails every week. One communication is a newsletter with updates on new locations in the works, introductions to new teachers and other studio-focused information. The other communication is a reminder that the next week's classes are opening for registration. Studio 2 has seen a drop off in immediate registrations following the "registration is open" email and instead experiences more last-minute sign-ups – something the business owners find frustrating from a sales projection and resource management standpoint.

Both studios could stand to improve their customer communications – both in terms of frequency and content. And they would also benefit from re-evaluating the platforms they're using to communicate, as not all customers rely on email as their primary source for information, particularly time-sensitive information. A more customer-centric look at their communications would likely drive increased open rates and engagement with the content, as well as support business goals.

If you're like these fitness studios and fall in either the under- or over-communicators categories, there's little risk of moving toward the middle. Considering your starting point, it's unlikely you'll allow yourself or your marketing team to veer too far in the other direction.

In today's technology-driven world, there's no excuse not to communicate. There are simply too many ways to keep in touch. From email to text messaging and social media messaging to the good old-fashioned telephone (yes, even land lines for some audiences) and handwritten notes, more than ample opportunity exists to keep in touch with your customers. It's a matter of choosing the right platforms, identifying the right frequency, and creating the right content to deliver the information your customers want and need. While this chapter focuses on outbound communications and customer support, there's plenty more in the next chapter on content and in chapter 13 on feedback.

Platform: What Method is Best to Communicate?

As with most recommendations in this book, the answer depends on your business and your customers. For businesses whose customers are millennials or teens, text messaging and in-app communications are far more likely to resonate and drive response than letters or even email. For older, more affluent audiences, a phone call may prove most impactful. Not sure how your customers want to hear from you? Ask!

You can also take into consideration how customers buy. This is often a good indicator. Online shoppers tend to prefer online communications, whereas bricks and mortar buyers may prefer a handwritten note or phone call.

Consider varying your communications and platforms to connect with customers in multiple ways. Different types of programs benefit from different platforms. For example, personalized "thank you for your business" communications will demand a different format (like a handwritten note) than a mass distribution monthly email newsletter.

Whatever platforms you choose, however, they require ongoing attention. Communications are a two way street. If you use email as a primary means of sending information to customers, you must also respond through this channel. And if you have a telephone number, a voicemail box that accepts messages is must, as is a commitment to checking the messages and returning the calls. There's nothing more frustrating for a customer than attempting to contact a small business – and getting zero response in return. So resist the urge to fill up a business card, email footer, or website contact us page with every possible method of communication. Instead focus on those channels that make sense for your customers and that you plan to use for customer engagement. (There's more on this topic in the next chapter.)

Timing & Frequency: When And How Often Should You Communicate?

Again, it depends. I like to think of it like Goldilocks and the Three Bears. The bed that was perfect for Papa Bear was far too hard for Goldilocks. And the one that made Mama Bear sleep tight was way too soft for Goldilocks' liking. But the Baby Bear's bed, now that was just right. The same thing goes for the frequency of communications for your business. While it might be just right for one business to send its customers a weekly text alert of new inventory, for others, an annual email reminder of an upcoming appointment may be more appropriate. The key is determining what makes the most sense to support your customer needs and business goals.

As you plan your communications schedule, focus on striking a balance between communicating frequently enough to stay top of mind and communicating too frequently and being annoying. It is highly possible that a customer might miss one communication or another, so regular contact and reminders help to get your message across and get customers the information they need.

Also consider your timing to both enhance the value of your message and avoid a negative reaction. This does not mean pinpointing the optimal hour or day for high email open rates. It means considering when a message is most valuable or most relevant.

Timing is important as you want to send your message with sufficient time for the customer to take action, but not so much lead time that they put it off until later. The goal is to give customers every chance to engage with your communications and give your programs every chance to be successful. Again, it's a balancing act and one that is specific to your business.

Sometimes, optimizing communications also means tweaking your scheduling or adjusting a message to meet the needs or consider the perspective of recipients.

For example, the agency we use to find a new au pair every year sends out a regular family email newsletter. They tie the content into the season by providing ideas for fun seasonal activities for au pairs, kids and families to do together, and they spotlight noteworthy participants in the program. It's typically a great email filled with relevant information.

However during the summer of 2015, a major technology meltdown at the US State Department completely halted the issuing of visas worldwide. Au pairs scheduled to arrive in the US were delayed and the few that were visiting their home countries and needed a visa renewal were stuck.

During this stressful time for families suddenly left without childcare, the agency sent out its summer newsletter. Though the issue impacted only 5% of its customers, the newsletter focused on sunshine and vacationing with your au pair, never once mentioning the issue and how the agency was helping impacted families (ours included). Those affected customers were left feeling unloved and that their issues were of no concern to the agency – something that could have been easily avoided with the addition of a short sidebar comment or even holding back the newsletter for a week to gather more information.

Content: What Should You Communicate?

This section goes hand-in-hand with the next chapter, which is dedicated entirely to content marketing and social media. One-to-one (individual) or one-to-many (mass) communications are equally important. Both must extend beyond sales-oriented and business-focused content to be relevant and valuable to customers.

As I already mentioned, it's absolutely ok to sell and inform through communications – both en masse and one-on-one. Making communications customer-centric is not about the message itself, but rather in the approach and positioning of that message. Rather than pushing a new offering or publishing a generic sales message, instead focus on how your product or service meets a customer need or solves a problem they're facing. Frame your message around an understanding of their situation. That's customer-centric communication – and it's more likely to generate a response.

The Bushcamp Company: Creating Truly Special Once in a Lifetime Experiences

"It doesn't cost money to listen to people and pay attention. Customer service is about making the customer feel seen."

- Andy Hogg, managing director,
The Bushcamp Company

"Did You Know?"

These three simple words provide the backbone for The Bushcamp Company's communications program and the entire Bushcamp experience, a high-end safari offering in Zambia.

"Did You Know?" started as a simple email program. Bushcamp's weekly message includes a fact about an animal, information about the environment, and/or exciting news about Bushcamp. While the content is varied, all messages are short, quick reads accompanied by a noteworthy photograph, often one that is provided by a guest. The email doesn't include a sales pitch or call to action – messages are intended to engage and keep Bushcamp top of mind.

These messages remind former guests of their beautiful experience, entice potential visitors to make a trip, and keep Bushcamp in touch with travel agents, who directly influence many of the Bushcamp's bookings. Without exception, Bushcamp receives numerous replies to each message, and when Andy makes sales calls to travel agents in the US, they comment on how much they love it.

But the weekly email is only one component of the company's communications strategy to gather information and customize the guest experience. Andy believes there's no such thing as too much guest contact. He's out front, engaging with guests from the moment they arrive and throughout their entire stay – asking about their day's experiences and making mental notes of the little details, an approach that is embraced by and expected of all team members.

Each morning, the Bushcamp team meets to review all guest arrivals and departures, requests and feedback. They make plans for special accommodations and personal touches based on notes they've taken in conversations with customers. The company lives by the notion that a personalized experience isn't hard, it's simply a matter of paying attention to the details and listening to people. For Bushcamp, that starts during the booking process when guests are asked many questions to get a sense of trip expectations and to find out if the guest is celebrating anything special.

For example, Andy tells a story of a time when two guests arrived exhausted after a long-haul flight. A manager overheard the woman comment to her husband, "I really just want beans on toast for dinner." When their dinner arrived, they were served the regular meal, plus beans on toast. The guest was moved to tears and the stage was set for a fabulous experience.

Bushcamp's philosophy is to "never say no to guests unless it's a matter of safety." Andy notes, "The fact is, making things special isn't expensive. We're feeding guests anyway. It's usually just logistics and sometimes a few pennies for gas to make the 'specials' happen. Emails don't cost anything, either. It's just a few extra minutes that make a huge difference."

And specials are a regular part of every Bushcamp experience. Every guest gets one "special" – a pop-up breakfast in the bush, a make-your-own pizza in the wild, or a lantern-lit drink at sunset by the river. While returning guests may expect something special, they will never have the same experience twice. Because Bushcamp not only listens, they also remember – documenting details of each guest's trip so that they can craft a new, exciting experience. Details are also shared with the booking travel agent so they can follow up with their clients after the trip and gain a better sense of the overall experience to share with other potential guests.

Bushcamp also takes customer engagement to social media. They post on Facebook multiple times a day to share the safari experience with former guests and those who (like me!) aspire to visit one day. Some images are captured by guides, but many are contributed by guests. And they also share images of the specials – something that former guests connect with and often comment on how meaningful the experience was for them – even years beyond their visit.

Bushcamp is quick to note that they operate in a highly competitive, tough business. But through their "Did You Know?" communications program, attention to detail, focus on active listening, and commitment to customer engagement, the business has differentiated itself and thrived when competitors have struggled.

Company Information and Updates

While you definitely want to sell and inform, email newsletters that offer nothing more than a direct-to-inbox version of your brochure are sure to deliver more unsubscribes than sales. Keeping customers up to date on new offerings, special events, and business updates can be relevant, valuable and customer-centric. Focus on keeping customers in the loop so they can make more informed purchases and learn about the products or services you offer. But to truly build a deeper relationship, communications must provide value to your customer – doing more than only selling.

Customer Support

When you connect with customers after their purchase, you give yourself an opportunity to check in on their satisfaction and provide proactive tips on getting the most from the product.

For example, a few years ago I purchased a bedwetting alarm for one of my kids who was working on staying dry overnight. The online retailer that had been essentially anonymous to me quickly became a trusted business. They connected with me, established a relationship, and turned into my top choice for medical supplies (should the need arise).

The day the product was delivered, I received an email with tips for getting my child engaged and comfortable with the alarm. Then, a week later, a second email came with encouragement and tips for sticking with the process, as it can sometimes be frustrating at first for kids and parents alike. A final "check in" message came about two weeks after that. These emails were canned and automated, of course, but the schedule and information was customized for me. Not a single message contained a sales pitch or upsell. PS – Please don't tell my kids I shared this story!

Proactive Reminders

When's the last time you asked your customers, "Is there anything else you need?" This type of communication falls in the same bucket as the familiar 6-month check-up reminder postcard that has long been the practice of dental offices. Communications in this category also take the form of gentle upsells, such as, "Did you know we offered <insert your service or product here>?"

Being proactive about your customers' potential needs helps to make sure that when new or recurring needs arise, your business is the default answer. Otherwise, customers may not know about your additional offerings that could benefit them (marketing fail on many levels!), or they may buy from another business that happens to be more top of mind when the need presents.

For example, The Shop Salon in Bethesda, MD takes a proactive approach to reminders. They email me six weeks after my previous appointment with a link to rebook. Without fail, I'm either already having a lousy hair day or know that one is coming soon. While automated, the reminder isn't pushy or salesy. Instead, they show me that they appreciate my business and they make my life easier – my next appointment is only a click away.

Thank You

As children, we were taught to say please and thank you. In small business, the value of communicating appreciation cannot be overstated. This is one category where I love going old school. Make a phone call or send a handwritten note just to say, "Thank you for doing business with us. We appreciate your confidence and trust in us, and we look forward to the opportunity to exceed your expectations."

THE BOTTOM LINE

Strong communications lie at the heart of every strong relationship, including those with customers. Small businesses must keep in touch with customers to stay top of mind, keep them informed, and support their needs. Beyond customer service and sales messages, however, communications empower businesses to reinforce their commitment to and understanding of customers. Effective communications do not depend on the platform you use or the automation you take advantage of. The tools are only the means to the end. Identifying the appropriate frequency, content and customization of your message to directly support customer engagement empowers effective communications and builds strong customer relationships.

CHAPTER 11

SOCIAL MEDIA & CONTENT MARKETING

"Social media – oh, our intern handles that." Eek!

Small businesses all too often turn over their most outward-facing communications to an underpaid college student with only marginal commitment to the business, the brand, and most concerning, the customers.

Blogs? They often fall by the wayside due to daily pressing business needs. While all the rage, social media and content marketing are among the most misunderstood, underestimated and under-resourced marketing tactics around.

As often as I hear small business owners speak of their intern-managed Facebook pages, I also read entrepreneurship how-tos that proclaim blogs and Facebook are absolute musts for every small business. After all, they're supposedly free and easy ways to preach to the masses. No. Definitely no. Throw out those myths now. Social media and content marketing encompass multiple platforms and many opportunities. They most definitely are not free. And embracing a push-only content strategy will result in little value to your customers.

Social media and content marketing are just like every other marketing tactic – you must evaluate each opportunity based on whether it is appropriate for your business, relevant to your customers, and a valuable expenditure of your marketing dollars. And to be effective, social media and content marketing programs must be planned for, integrated with other marketing efforts, and focused on engaging your customers – not preaching to them. (I group social media and content marketing together in this chapter, because social media is often mostly content driven.)

Perhaps most importantly for small businesses, social media offers an incredible channel for customer engagement and customer service – allowing you to connect and communicate with customers in a forum they're already comfortable with and using regularly. A platform that encourages quick response, social media allows you to quickly and efficiently address questions and complaints, provide customer support, book appointments and even deliver customer love. And it provides customers with an easy way to engage with your business – leading to greater sales, a higher close rate and increased customer satisfaction.

CHOOSING PLATFORMS

There is no one social media platform that is a must-have for every small business – any one of the many already out there or coming online seemingly everyday can be valuable. Choose what works best for you based on how you want to communicate with your customers, as well as which platforms your customers both frequent on a regular basis and turn to for information about the products or services you offer. The key to success isn't the platforms you choose but rather putting them to work for you to engage and connect with customers.

The value of social media can be huge, but there is risk, too. Whether you utilize Facebook, Instagram, Pinterest, Twitter,

LinkedIn, Snapchat or any other platform, you must commit to being responsive and accessible via the channel. If you fail to engage quickly (fast replies are expected), you run the risk of frustrating customers, losing sales as your customers turn to competitors for answers or, worse, receiving complaints about your lack of responsiveness publicly on social media. Failure to engage can also call the status of your business into question – leaving would-be customers to guess whether or not you're even still open for business.

I offer the example of a community hospital that undertook a substantial construction endeavor – the renovation of its existing facility as well as a significant addition of new square footage. The hospital is situated adjacent to a residential community, and residents were not happy about the expansion and associated noise and disruption from the effort. Seeking to keep neighbors apprised of project status, upcoming work and changes to plans in real-time, the hospital took to Twitter. The platform was theoretically a great choice – residents were squarely in the demographic of Twitter's user base and the platform made it easy to deliver updates and information in a timely manner. There was just one problem: the hospital never responded to tweets or direct messages. As a result, the community was even more frustrated and felt the hospital showed little care for their concerns.

Be selective in the platforms you choose. Leverage only the ones that support your business goals and your customer engagement strategy... and that you will use on daily basis. The biggest mistake most small businesses make is setting up a profile and forgetting about it. You'd never ignore calls or emails, right? Social media inquiries demand the same responsiveness – only faster.

CONTENT PLANNING & EXECUTION

On the push content front, whether you're posting in 140-character snippits on Twitter or long-form blog posts on your own website, it's all content. There is tons of information already out there on content marketing. The recommendations are pretty consistent and I agree with them:

- Be relevant by complementing sales and company-centric information with value-added content that is interesting to customers.

- Implement a content calendar to plan for posts in advance.

- Utilize images and video wherever possible.

- Strive for shares over likes.

- Help like-minded and interested individuals find your content by using hashtags.

All true and all useful advice when it comes to planning content. I'll leave the details on content generation to the many books and thousands of articles dedicated entirely to this topic. Instead, I want to look at content marketing from the customer standpoint – what value does each area provide to your business as it relates to your customers?

As is my recommendation for all marketing programs, content marketing should be rooted in a strong plan that supports business objectives and considers your customer and audience. And the plan must provide for flexibility to accommodate new opportunities as they present and to adapt to the communications climate as it changes.

Content marketing is often most powerful when it is less scripted. The social media posts that resonate the strongest with customers are the ones that come from the heart and capture the moment. So for as much as you plan, don't be afraid to post ad hoc, in-the-moment content.

A note of caution when it comes to social media and content marketing – they require perhaps more situational awareness and adaptation than any other element of marketing. Posts are immediately visible to customers alongside everything else happening in the world. And news events – both positive and negative – happen on a world stage and impact how your content is received.

These days, it feels like there are more crisis situations occurring than ever before. And because of the 24-hour news cycle and constant access to information, it is expected that your content will be sensitive to and considerate of the situation of the day. Those not in business likely don't realize you have planned and scheduled posts weeks in advance. So be sure that as you plan and automate your content, that you stay on top of any breaking news and edit your posts accordingly. The last thing you want is to inadvertently offend customers or for your business to appear insensitive because what had been a benign post wasn't canceled in a timely manner.

CONTENT – FROM A CUSTOMER PERSPECTIVE
Self-Promotional

Business-centric content that focuses on your events, sales, products and other promotions can be highly relevant to customers. Self-promotional content doesn't have to be limited to "buy" messages, though. It can also give your customers a deeper understanding of your business, employees, values and customer engagement.

Social media is a great place to highlight customer accolades, share photos of you engaging with customers, and showcase in-person customer events. You can also use social media to give your customers behind-the-scenes looks at a new product in development, congratulate employees on achievements, and highlight community service efforts. Each of these content types further educates customers about your business and creates a stronger personal connection to your business.

Thought Leadership

Social media and content marketing offer a unique way to demonstrate your understanding of your industry while supporting your customers' need for relevant information. But you don't have to constantly create original content to do so.

By curating others' content and sharing it through your own channels, you help customers easily keep up with information and resources that are valuable – and that they probably don't have time to dig for. (Curating = reading other people's stuff on a particular topic and sharing what you deem most relevant to your customers and your audience.) Content may come from mainstream media, bloggers or others in your industry – anyone writing on or talking about the topic.

Plus, when you add your own two cents to the conversation, you further customers' understanding of your perspective and approach, as well as position yourself as a thought leader on the subject. Your color commentary can be as short as a sentence added to a retweet or as long as a thoughtful blog post filled with your take on the subject at hand.

Borrowed Relevance

Holidays and "holidays" (like National Popcorn Day!) offer a way to associate your business with something beyond your brand. Use these dates to showcase your business's personality and passions, and create connections on topics that interest both your business and your customers. Plus, posting lighthearted content is a great way to break up your customers' news feeds.

If you go down this road, however, make sure your content is interesting, relevant and specific to your business. Generic Happy 4th of July messages rarely generate any customer engagement. Likewise clip art or memes lifted from Google don't do anything to demonstrate your business's patriotism. And you definitely never want to force a holiday that isn't relevant to your business – even if it is potentially of interest to your customers. I still cringe when I think about the yoga studio that offered new customers a package discount linked with September 11th and promoted via a social media campaign – 9+11 = 20% off! Appalling.

Instead, find the holidays and "holidays" that make sense for your brand. I love the campaign run by a professional organizer who showcased a different photo of a favorite organizational product or well-organized space every day of Get Organized Month. Every photo was provided by customers. Relevant, customer-centric, engaging and visual.

Your small businesses can also borrow relevance by associating with the news of the day. However, this is another area where caution is warranted and the connections must be relevant.

For example, I love the campaign that DC Access, a local internet service provider in Washington DC, ran on the day the Metro shut down for safety checks and repairs. While the city was literally brought to a screeching halt due to lack of public transportation, DC Access encouraged customers to share photos of how their connectivity allowed them to maintain productivity as they worked from home. A random winner was selected from the photos submitted to win a free month of service.

On the flip side, my stomach turned over when I saw a cooking website post a recipe for energy-building oatmeal for first responders supporting the Boston Marathon bombing. Forced relevance, insensitive and entirely business-centric.

Customer-Contributed

Perhaps the most engaging of all social media activities is the content created and contributed by your customers themselves. Encourage your customers to get social with you! Ask them to submit photos for contests, tweet their experience with a particular situation, or give them the opportunity to take over your social feeds for a day. When customers participate in your marketing – social or otherwise – they feel more connected to your business and engaged in your success. Plus, the multiplier effect of reaching their networks can't be beat.

The Bottom Line

By all means, use your intern to help you execute – but not outright own – your social media and content marketing. Empower them to engage with customers by providing guidance and direction for the social media program. Evaluate and implement social media and content marketing as you would any other marketing program, with a focus on goals, a plan for execution, and a customer's lens for evaluation. The keys to social media and content marketing success lie in your ability to utilize the many platforms available to your small business to connect with customers. Social media as a free billboard simply doesn't work. So...

- Determine which platforms make sense for your business and your customers – you don't have to be on all of them, no matter what is deemed "most established" or "must have" on any given the day. This includes Facebook.

- Be present only on the platforms you can and will commit to managing regularly – not just pushing content out, but engaging with and responding to customers, too.

- Develop a content plan that is representative of your brand and interesting to customers. Then, layer in ad hoc posts often.

- Adapt, adapt, adapt. Avoid missteps by keeping a constant eye on feedback and the world happening around you.

- Share! And share again. There's no value in content that no one reads.

Chapter 12

Get People Talking: Referrals & Word Of Mouth

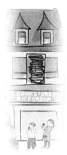

"I don't do any marketing. All of my new business comes from referrals."

How often do small business owners make this claim? I hear it all the time, particularly from service providers like life coaches, attorneys and physicians. Referrals often make the best customers as they come from those who already know and understand your business. As a result, your referral customers are more likely to mirror your existing ideal customers.

But referrals don't generate themselves. Referrals happen because your business consistently delivers an experience that customers appreciate, recognize and want to share with others. Every project you deliver on time and every product that performs as promised is marketing. Every urgent situation you address with calm and grace and every time you exceed customer expectations – it's all marketing.

While these basics are minimum standards that all businesses of any size should follow, the plethora of negative online reviews indicate that's sadly not the case. So for a customer-centric business that depends on word of mouth for growth, delivering as promised, on time, or at a fair price should only be the beginning of getting customers talking. Valuable peer endorsements are earned. And this applies to product companies as much as service-based businesses.

> **"**
>
> Referrals happen because your business consistently delivers an experience that customers appreciate, recognize and want to share with others. Every project you deliver on time and every product that performs as promised is marketing.

There are three primary paths toward referrals for small businesses.

1. *Be top of mind when referable moments occur.*

More often than not, you won't be around the office water cooler, on the community listserv, at the playground, or at a networking event when someone asks, "Do you know anyone who sells [insert the product or service you offer]?" Many referrals happen when you aren't present to jump up and down shouting, "YES! We do/sell that!"

Would-be customers turn to family, friends, peers, communities and networks for everything from hotels in Paris to a career counselor to the best stroller for a growing toddler. Through regular, ongoing communications, you keep your business top of mind as the obvious solution to the challenge or frustration that is being discussed over a glass of wine or at the park. Through these communications, as well as excellent customer service, product performance, or other noteworthy interaction with your business, you secure your place in the conversation.

The perfect case in point is Adelso Ceron, a residential painter who I've not only used many times myself, but also referred to others on many occasions. Why does this solopreneur without a website or email list stay on my go-to list? He stands out by showing up when he says he will, finishing a job within the agreed-upon timeline, doing consistently good work, offering fair pricing, and using only high-quality products. And he's a friendly, genuinely nice person. Adelso makes an impression through the basics of good ol' fashioned customer service. Referral opportunity gained.

2. Create referable moments.

When you engage your customers with unique marketing programs and shower customers with love, you get people talking. You create a referable moment.

Whether it's an awesome customer experience, a remarkable customer engagement program, or a noteworthy advertising campaign, you earn the opportunity to drive the conversation. The goal is the unsolicited tweet that goes something like, "OMG, @RealEstateAgent. What a fabulous welcome to our new home. Thank you!" Or the girls' night out conversation that starts with, "Have you been to XYZ restaurant recently? You should see how they've made waiting for a table more fun."

In chapter 14, I'll go into more detail about how to make customer love a regular part of your business. To get people talking, you need to do the unexpected. When you surprise your clients with flowers on their birthdays, cookies on Valentine's Day, or the perfect sentiment just when they need a pick me up, they're certain to sing your praises and share with their friends about the fabulous relationship they have with you. What happens next? Referrals commence.

I can't tell you how many public social media thank you messages we receive each year when we send our clients boxes of Girl Scout Cookies for Valentine's Day. Clients often tell us how the cookies surprised and excited them – sparking conversations with their husband/wife, friends, and colleagues about the unexpected gift.

3. Ask.

When's the last time you asked for a referral? Ask your customers, "Is there anyone else that you know that should know about us?" Don't be afraid to ask. Your happy customers would love to share you with their friends and networks. But, remember, like you, they're busy with their own lives. So giving referrals isn't always top of mind unless someone asks (#1) or you encourage it through being awesome (#2). Be sure to make it a real ask, not just a tag in your email footer (a common practice particularly for real estate agents and financial advisors) that often goes unnoticed.

Let's set aside a huge myth – asking for referrals absolutely does not make you look desperate for business! It simply tells your customers that you appreciate working with them and others like them, and that you're excited to work with or serve those they know. Plus, your loyal, engaged customers are excited for your business growth. Getting to be a part of this success by referring others reinforces their role in your journey. Everyone likes feeling connected to a winning team.

"Acts" of Customer Love Pay Off

One sleepless night, Amy found inspiration in a documentary about obesity in America and made a life change that would lead her down the path of entrepreneurship.

Drawing on her background in business and theater, Amy decided to launch a juice bar that also offers home delivery service, a concept found on nearly every corner in New York City and throughout California but completely missing in her area. Over time, she expanded the menu to include smoothies and a selection of vegan food.

Amy recognizes that many don't typically think of theater experience as a strong asset to bring to business, but she disagrees, commenting, "There's so much going on behind the scenes – backstage – we couldn't function on stage without it." And drawing on acting skills when it comes to putting on a smile when dealing with an overly demanding or unpleasant customer definitely comes in handy.

Amy is passionate about empowering her customers to live a healthy lifestyle and to provide greater access to locally pressed, unpasteurized, truly raw juices. To this end, the company commits to having juices on home delivery customers' doorsteps by 8:30 am. However, one regular customer insisted he needed delivery by 6 am. Considering the customer's close proximity to their retail store, Amy chose to oblige this request (essentially a demand, as she tells it). She adjusted the store's morning delivery route from her production facility so the first drop would be at the customer's home – moving the drop-off of daily inventory at the retail store to the second stop. When they discovered that the customer's driveway was long, narrow and unable to accommodate the delivery truck, Amy's team parked at the bottom and walked the juice to the door.

A year later, the customer love Amy literally delivered proved invaluable in the way of a great referral. Amy learned that this demanding customer was the president of a large, local retailer. The company was expanding its wellness offerings and building out its on-site food program to provide healthier options. At his recommendation, she was invited to establish an on-site retail location to serve both visitors and staff.

Week after week, Amy and her team went above and beyond for this customer. Was it marketing? For sure. Though she never thought of it that way.

Say Thank You

When it comes to customers who come by way of referral, handle with care. While you should be striving for excellence with all of your customer relationships, referrals should take that commitment to a higher level. When a customer shares your business with a friend, they're standing behind you and implying that they trust your work, product or experience enough to attach their name to yours. Respect this confidence that they're placing in you.

Also, don't forget your manners! Say thank you. And when it's appropriate, keep the referring customer posted on that status of a referral (not the details, but a quick update that you will or will not be working with the individual they sent your way). A thank you can take the form of a phone call, a handwritten note or a token gift. If you go down the gift path, make sure that it is appropriate considering your business and customer.

For example, don't be like the Lasik eye surgery center that tried to entice patients to refer others with an offer of a $25 gas card. The offer felt cheap considering that the procedure costs thousands of dollars and is not covered by insurance. Plus, there was no logical connection between the offer and the business.

On the positive side, consider the financial advisor who makes a donation to a nonprofit or charity of the referring client's choosing to demonstrate appreciation and to show support for their interests. Because he manages significant wealth for clients, a financial incentive simply doesn't feel right.

I also really like the Uber model that is used by many app-based and online companies. Both the referring customer and new customer receive a financial incentive to patronize the business. Everybody wins!

> " When you engage your customers with unique marketing programs and shower customers with love, you get people talking. You create a referable moment.

WORD OF MOUTH:
ON ENDORSEMENTS, TESTIMONIALS & ONLINE REVIEWS

Beyond one-to-one referrals, word of mouth can directly influence both buzz building for a new business and ongoing growth for an existing one. In the age of Amazon reviews, Google My Business, Yelp, and Facebook commentary, reviews are no longer only for restaurants and yoga studios. Product and service companies alike can substantially benefit from customer kudos. And they can experience irreparable harm from negative feedback – regardless of whether or not it's legitimate.

Call them testimonials, reviews, or even case studies (for B2B and B2C), online endorsements can provide a significant level of comfort for a prospect or would-be buyer. The business impact of these reviews is real. According to market research conducted by British local search company, BrightLocal, 92 percent of Internet users read reviews in order to determine the quality of a local business.[6] Respondents also indicate that they trust reviews as much as they do personal recommendations from friends and family.

While even the most satisfied customers – your raving fans – may be singing your praises to their family and friends, they may not think to provide this public endorsement. So, again, ask! Follow up on a positive email interaction and ask, "Would you be willing to provide a testimonial about your experience with us?" Or include this request in a new customer email series. Anytime your customer gives you positive feedback is an opportunity to ask for them to share this sentiment more publicly.

Once you have the kudos, don't forget to share them! Testimonials are great for websites, social media posts, brochure fodder, and RFP responses.

THE BOTTOM LINE

Do what you say you're going to do, leave customers happy, and they will refer and share positive feedback. While they sometimes need a little encouragement or a reminder, when you have strong relationships and satisfied customers, they often pay in ways far beyond the balance on their invoices. Your strong, customer-centric foundation lies at the heart of a word of mouth-driven business.

While you likely won't be present at the moment when a referral occurs, there are three ways you can impact these business-growing customer shares.

- Be top of mind when referable moments occur.

- Create referable moments.

- Ask.

And remember that in today's era of the highly connected customer, online reviews are a critical part of word of mouth marketing. Encourage your happy customers to help build buzz for your business by sharing their kudos online.

Chapter 13

The Power Of Customer Feedback

Your customer's perspective offers an invaluable resource for continuously improving and maintaining excellence. This entire book is about developing stronger relationships with your customers, creating more valuable interactions with prospects and connecting with both customers and prospects in ways that resonate deeply. So, how do you know what they want?

First, ask! Customers who already love you are happy to give feedback about how you are rocking their world and where you have room for improvement. Engaged, loyal customers care about your success, and their feedback can prove vital in providing direction for the business. Because dissatisfied customers don't always share their frustrations without prompting, you need to ask.

Second, listen when unhappy customers talk. With a good understanding of their perspective, you are empowered to work toward earning back their trust and confidence, not just resolving the immediate situation.

Asking for Feedback

Before you sign up for SurveyMonkey, assemble a customer advisory board, or give your employees three questions to ask after each sale, decide what information you're trying to gather and how you intend to use it. Whether you're looking to secure insights on customer satisfaction, interest in a new product or service, or feedback on a new name or location, consider the customers' point of view when designing your research.

Respect Customers' Time

If you're asking customers to give you feedback, be sure to respect their time. Ask only questions that provide valuable insights and skip the ones that offer only marginal value or don't really qualify the data. Even seemingly quick questions can add up to a lot of time, leading customers to bail out before they complete a survey. Make "nice to have" but not essential questions non-mandatory. And if you're asking questions in a focus group or advisory board setting, running too long can result in participant boredom or frustration that they've committed too much time to the effort.

Be Open to Feedback

Customer feedback can validate ideas, but it can also offer eye-opening perspective that can be tough to swallow. If you ask for feedback, be open to it – positive, negative or somewhere in the middle. Don't try to convince a customer that you're right. When asking for feedback, it isn't the time to respond defensively or with "Yes, I hear you, but…" If you don't intend to use the feedback you receive or aren't in a place to be open to hearing it, don't ask. This isn't fair to customers, and it can have the opposite of the desired effect – leaving them feeling bullied or their perspective unvalued.

A few years ago, I facilitated a customer advisory board for a small professional services business. The program provided highly relevant feedback to the business owner, as participants systematically evaluated several areas of business operations over a one-year period. While the business owner received reports after each board meeting and made several business decisions based on the feedback, he was never in the room at the meetings. Instead, I conveyed his appreciation and updates to participants. I highly recommend this approach, as it can be extremely hard as a business owner to be impartial in this type of setting.

At the conclusion of the year, the business owner and I both took the customer board members out for a private dining experience at a nice local restaurant to thank them for their time and candor. The conversation eventually moved on from the niceties to the participants directly asking the business owner for his feedback on the value of the effort. He did a great job of expressing his appreciation and sharing both changes he was making and some he wasn't despite their recommendations.

Unfortunately, he also got defensive when they asked questions about his decision-making process. They weren't questioning him – they were simply asking questions to understand. While he caught himself and moved quickly back to appreciation and explanation, it was a good reminder for us both on the importance of taking constructive criticism in the positive manner in which it is intended.

When Things Go Wrong

Even the most customer-centric businesses can have dissatisfied customers. Businesses are run by humans. Humans are imperfect. Sometimes they make mistakes. Sometimes these mistakes impact a single customer and sometimes an entire segment gets a raw deal. No matter how hard you work to avoid a bad situation, sometimes it happens. And feedback from these less happy customers is just as valuable as the guidance you receive from the elated ones. While it can feel like unhappy customers are quick to complain and share their (sometimes less than constructive) feedback, research indicates that many more dissatisfied customers don't say a word.[7] Silence is not a win when it comes to an unhappy customer. You don't have the opportunity to address the situation with the individual and make improvements to help prevent it from happening with others down the road.

When customers take the time to share that things didn't go as expected, they give you the opportunity to make it up to them and to make things right. They give you a second chance – a chance to turn a complaint into a customer engagement opportunity. When things go wrong, listen first. Hear what customers have to say and work to understand how they feel. Then, take responsibility and work to resolve the situation. While bad situations aren't always your fault, they are your problem… and your opportunity. In other words, negative feedback gives you a chance to convert an unhappy customer into an advocate.

One of my favorite examples involving customer feedback is an experience I had with a small Oregon ice cream company, Alden's Ice Cream. I stopped into my local grocery to pick up vanilla ice cream to go with a delicious summer berry pie I was bringing to a friend's for dessert. I grabbed a half-gallon of Alden's, a brand I'd never heard of, but was on sale. At checkout, I was surprised to learn that vanilla actually wasn't on sale despite the fact that all other flavors were marked at a discount. The cashier gave me what I later learned was incorrect information.

Because I was in a rush, I bought the ice cream anyway and tweeted my frustration. Alden's immediately responded, apologized and asked for my address to make it up to me. A week later, five coupons for ice cream arrived in my mailbox.

I again took to Twitter, but this time to offer accolades. I've not only used my coupons, but bought the product many times since. Alden's turned a bad first impression into a positive customer experience by accepting responsibility and apologizing even though it wasn't their fault.

On the flip sign, sometimes, things go wrong and it's the customer's fault. Just as businesses are run by people who make mistakes, customers are people who make mistakes, too. Perhaps a customer failed to read the menu carefully or reveal that they have a dairy allergy, and their salad arrived with feta cheese. Or maybe they didn't pay close attention to the cancellation policy for an appointment they'd made, didn't show up, and were charged anyway. In these situations, customers are cranky because things didn't go according to their expectations.

Whether the fault in a bad situation lies with a product failure, poor service, distributor issues or customer misunderstanding, take the high road. You have the ability to manage how the situation is handled and impact how the customer feels after the interaction. So, apologize for the bad experience no matter who is at fault, make amends when appropriate, and generally help the customer through the situation. Ask questions to get to the bottom of where the breakdown occurred. Let the customer be heard. Even if the customer is at fault and concessions aren't warranted, a smile and sympathetic approach can go far in remedying the situation.

Respond, Respond, Respond.

Even when you don't ask, feedback can often find its way to you – and not always in ways you like. In the last chapter we talked about the positive power of social media platforms and online review sites in generating buzz and word of mouth to help grow your business. But certainly the power of these platforms cuts both ways.

Beyond receiving feedback, social media platforms also present an awesome opportunity to demonstrate how you handle different situations. Your response to both positive and negative comments on these publicly facing platforms allows you to showcase your customer service – giving would-be customers a glimpse into how they'd be treated as customers themselves. So while you may take a conversation offline to remedy a situation or satisfy a disgruntled customer, be sure to respond publicly on the platform where an inquiry was received as well. This lets the commenting individual and the world know that you are responsive and addressing the concern or are appreciative of positive feedback.

With these platforms, response time is critical. There's an expectation of near immediacy. Facebook even tells users how fast a page responds to inquiries, at least as of this writing. In chapter 11, I recommended that you only utilize the social media platforms on which you can commit to regularly engaging. However, you also need to keep a constant eye on your online profile. Beyond the social media platforms you've chosen to utilize, Google, Yelp, TripAdvisor and many others allow and encourage reviews regardless of whether you've taken time to optimize your business profile or strategically chosen to utilize it for marketing and customer communications. So keep on top of your online presence. You don't want to be caught off guard by a negative review or disappointed customer that could have been easily addressed but went unanswered for months simply because you weren't paying attention.

"
When customers take the time to share that things didn't go as expected, they give you the opportunity to make it up to them and to make things right. They give you a second chance – a chance to turn a complaint into a customer engagement opportunity.

USING FEEDBACK FOR CONTINUOUS IMPROVEMENT

While the majority of this chapter is focused on handling complaints, not all feedback is negative, particularly when it comes from your most loyal customers. Sometimes feedback takes the form of new product ideas, ways to deliver a service, menu items or more. This feedback is among the most valuable of the comments you receive.

When you use customer feedback to develop new offerings, update policies, or make any other business change, be sure to update your audience and let them know where the idea came from. Customers love to be heard, and even if the idea wasn't theirs, you're reinforcing your customer-centric commitment by giving credit where credit is due. Plus, keeping customers apprised of developments and changes that are a result of customer feedback underscores your appreciation of all feedback and recognition of its value in your business. This further encourages customers to continue to provide this meaningful insight. For the customers' ideas you've implemented, be sure to follow up directly to close the loop and let them know their voice was heard.

NOT ALL FEEDBACK IS CREATED EQUAL

While I am a firm believer in considering all feedback, in some cases, it simply doesn't warrant significant attention or frustration.

Haters & Takers

There will always be haters. You can never please these customers. And there will always be takers who undervalue your offering or expect to be catered to at every step. This group often has plenty to say, but their feedback is rarely constructive. You can do your best to explain your policies, customize your products or make your business more accessible, but there are some people who are simply never satisfied. With this group, you can never win. The best you can do in this situation is to limit interaction as much as possible and remember that you aren't for everyone. These folks are not your customers. Focus your energy on positive customer relationships and those whose feedback provides real business value.

Online Trolls

If there's one group who can be 100 percent ignored, it's the nasty online trolls who hide behind anonymity and offer nothing but harsh, unwarranted, and often politically or emotionally motivated criticism. These folks are the ones who comment on or tweet in response to blogs and articles you publish with unfounded and uneducated claims or accusations. They have limited online followings and are looking for nothing more than a soapbox. Engaging in a dialogue with them will provide no value. As these aren't your customers and very likely aren't connected to your potential customers, you can safely ignore this feedback and not even respond or acknowledge the negativity.

One-Offs

In small business, it can often feel like everyone has an opinion on your products, your pricing, your location, your policies, your communications – you name it. Feedback will come from customers and prospects, partners and associates, even competitors and friends. But don't pivot and change business policies or direction based on each and every idea or criticism. If there's a common thread or consistent drumbeat of concern, then yes, take note. But if you adapt for every comment, you'll never gain traction on anything. And a change you make for one customer won't work for another.

Mom Doesn't Always Know Best

Is your mom, spouse, best friend or [insert other influencer in your life here] part of your target market? No? Ignore them. At least when it comes to their opinions on marketing your business. As a mother and daughter, I'd never suggest ignoring mom's sage wisdom on just about anything else!

My favorite story is that of an entrepreneur launching a new business in the wedding industry. She shared her beautiful logo designs and website photography with her mastermind group of talented, smart women. She got tons of feedback. The only challenge was that her business specifically targets men. While the insights were valuable in terms of providing a different perspective, they did little to consider the actual audience receiving the message.

So, while those closest to you might have great ideas, their perspectives are likely not useful unless they're grounded in some relevant experience or direct connection to your offering or target customer.

Creation Wines:
Ensuring Customers' Cups
Overfloweth

"A lot of small businesses (and big businesses) are afraid of getting feedback – negative or positive. For us, we see it as an opportunity to find out what's not working; it gives us the chance to fix it and make a customer like us again. If they don't complain, we simply won't know what's wrong."

Creations Wines knows its customer. And it knows its customers' likes, dislikes, wants and habits. How? The winery constantly asks for feedback on a variety of platforms, including email surveys, social media, and, most importantly, one-on-one in its South African tasting room. In fact, the winery hires employees based on passion for customer service. As a result, customers regularly engage, providing ideas, a fresh perspective, and candid, tough-to-hear criticism.

The winery watches as many other South African businesses in the tourism and hospitality industry view their customers as one-time visitors. But Carolyn Martin, owner of Creation Wines, sees things a different way. "We view every visitor as a customer. Period. It's not just about the one time they're in the tasting room. We sell a ton of cases to our guests for export overseas, and our customers drive tons of referrals. The return may come six months or six years down the road, but that's ok."

And their return on customer service has and continues to come – Creation Wines features notably high return visitor and referral rates. Its tasting room serves upwards of 50,000 customers each year and has become a destination in the area – success metrics the winery attributes entirely to the way it engages with customers.

Most importantly, however, Creation leverages the insights its customers share to refine the winery's offerings, including product, experience and communications strategies. In fact, it attributes some of its most successful new products and experiences directly to customer feedback.

For example, when a group of hunters wanted to come in at 9am – hours before the winery officially opened – Creation put together a special brunch for their group. The brunch worked out so well that breakfast has become a staple offering, filling the tasting room during a time when it was typically "dead quiet." And, based on feedback, Creation brought in tea, milk and juice to make the tasting room a friendlier place for expectant moms, those who don't drink, and families. By adding these offerings, they made it easier for all customers to participate in and enjoy the overall Creation Wines experience.

While the winery engages one-on-one in its tasting room, it credits social media and email marketing with providing some of its most glowing kudos, best ideas and candid criticisms. They note that online engagement offers a comfortable, easy way for customers to share feedback they might not otherwise express – both positive and negative. Creation's customers feel comfortable engaging through social media as the winery doesn't use it as an advertising platform. Rather, it focuses on publishing quality content that is driven by customer interests and presented in an interesting and timely way. Importantly, there's a constant reinforcement of Creation's commitment to answering questions, helping facilitate visits or purchases, and receiving feedback. The approach works – within 15 minutes of every email newsletter, the winery receives inquiries, questions and comments.

Carolyn offers a few tips on running a customer-feedback-driven small business:

Ask For the Feedback You Want

No matter how open your lines of customer communication or how customer-friendly your culture, sometimes people want to be specifically asked for their feedback. Sometimes, they expect you already know how they felt about an experience. Even though we're constantly engaging, we don't always know. So we ask customers in the tasting room for feedback, we email every first-time customer, and we send out surveys.

Takeaway: Give customers the opportunity to provide feedback, and give your business the opportunity to get the information you want and need.

Don't Be Afraid To Change Course

We try all kinds of new ideas based on customer feedback. Sometimes they work, sometimes not. But we're not afraid to try something new to meet a customer request, tweak something already in place to make it better, or kill a program if it's not working.

Takeaway: Go for it! As a small business you have the agility to make changes quickly.

Recognize That Not All Customers' Needs Are Equal

Our customers' needs are varied. That's why just as we have many different options for tastings and visits, we have many different options for customer communications and engagement. While we're more active on the mainstream social media platforms, we're on many others, too.

Takeaway: Make sure you connect with your customers on the platforms they use and are comfortable with.

Leverage Your Team

Every member of our 20-person team is encouraged to interact directly with customers – in person and online. They engage as themselves, not the official brand, but the association with the winery is clear. While there are risks, the payoff is very high. The engagement rings true to customers and feels special in that a real person – not just the company Twitter handle – cares enough to connect.

Takeaway: Empower your team to carry your customer torch.

THE BOTTOM LINE

Feedback isn't always easy to hear, but not hearing from unhappy or underwhelmed customers is far worse. Recognize both criticism and praise for the incredible value they offer so you can continue to improve on your business and customer service. And remember:

- Ask for feedback and use it for continuous improvement. Be willing to look honestly at your business and implement suggestions that make sense.

- Respond directly to both positive and negative unsolicited feedback on the platform on which it was received. Recognize and appreciate praise. Continue conversations offline when appropriate and necessary to address negative situations.

- Take the high road and maintain a positive conversation regardless of who is at fault in a negative situation – the goal is turning an unhappy customer into a happy one again.

- Remember that not all feedback is created equal and demands business change.

- Avoid knee-jerk reactions and never get defensive.

CHAPTER 14

CREATING CUSTOMER LOVE

While this entire book is about creating customer love, this chapter shines a spotlight on loving on your customers – going beyond your everyday customer-centric approach to creating those special "wow" moments. This is by far my favorite chapter, because customer love is my passion. Plus, loving on your customers is fun, rewarding and simply feels good. (Apologies in advance – I use the word "love" a lot in this chapter.)

User experience, or "UX," for online businesses, and customer experience, or "CX" for bricks and mortar or service-based ones, are all the rage in the business world. Customer love is more than a buzzword, though. It's about creating an experience that is truly memorable. Just as with many of the marketing ideas in this book, some customer love can be planned and consistent, while other customer love is off-the-cuff and customer specific. Though customer love doesn't feel like marketing, it very much is – it is core to your customers' relationships with your business. Customer love gets customers talking.

Maya Angelou said, "I've learned that people will forget what you said, people will forget what you did, but people will never forget how you made them feel." I couldn't agree more. This is true of both people and businesses. Customer love is all about making lasting positive impressions on customers.

Before I dive into a few of the many examples of customer love that inspire me and hopefully get you psyched up to love on your customers, I want to revisit a few of the concepts from section 1, as they apply strongly to customer love and definitely bear repeating.

- While every aspect of your business offers the opportunity to shower your customers with love, you don't have to embrace every opportunity. Pick and choose the places in your business where taking your engagement up a notch makes sense.

- Your partners, distributors, resellers and others in your channel are customers, too. Love on them as much as your end buyers. Sometimes more.

- Great customer connections happen one at a time. Customer love can be applied to a single customer, a handful of customers or everyone in your database. Just as not all customers are created equal and not all customers connect in the same way, some are more valuable than others. So the way in which you love on them doesn't always have to be equal across the board.

- Customer love doesn't have to be expensive. While many of the examples I highlight in this chapter include a gift of some kind, a handwritten note, a phone call, or a visit can be just as impactful. The connection is what matters, not the budget.

So where to love? The possibilities are endless.

Service Delivery

If you're a service provider, you can introduce love into your everyday operations by looking beyond policies and focusing on how your services fit into customers' lives. I love hearing about realtors who leave flowers and a "welcome home" note in the kitchens of their clients' new homes the day of settlement or college coaches and SAT prep tutors who send Bed, Bath & Beyond gift cards to their high school graduates to help them with dorm room essentials.

One of my favorite examples is a family photographer who frequently photographs newborn babies. Any moms reading this know that your hands aren't looking their best when you're changing diapers and doing nonstop baby laundry – never mind that those hectic early weeks leave no time for pampering. However, moms' hands show up often in photos. So once a photo shoot is confirmed, this photographer sends new moms a gift certificate for a manicure at a salon in their neighborhood so they can conveniently prepare for their photo session. This $20 investment generates significant returns in the customer love it creates. Money well spent!

CUSTOMER SERVICE

All too often, customer service means customer support. But it doesn't have to. Customer service goes well beyond answering the phone to address questions or problems. I've both experienced and heard stories of veterinarians who love on their customers – both the four-legged variety and their owners – by going above and beyond during the difficult and emotional process of putting a pet to sleep.

When my childhood dog, Kendra, slipped on the ice and was paralyzed at the age of 14, we were left with little choice. The veterinarian who had cared for her since she was a puppy opened the office on New Year's Eve without blinking an eye. Aside from the incredible support our family received that day, there was no charge for the emergency visit or the procedure.

BIRTHDAYS & ANNIVERSARIES

Showing customer love for birthdays and anniversaries never gets old. Everyone appreciates a little extra love on their birthday (particularly those tough milestone ones). And what newlywed couple celebrating their one-year anniversary wouldn't be happily surprised when their wedding planner recognizes the occasion?

One birthday-focused program I love is run by a baby boutique that celebrates its babies' first few birthdays. Because it works with parents to decorate nurseries and select baby gear, this retailer knows (at least approximately) when its smallest customers are born. To celebrate the occasion, the business sends the new little bundles a onesie, as well as birthday cards for their first three birthdays. The cards recognize mom and dad, too, but the cards are addressed to the kids. Parents love the gesture and the kids happily tear up the paper.

lil omm: Customer Love Beyond the Mat

"The yoga studio market is saturated. But being a caring, community-oriented yoga studio is not."

lil omm founder Pleasance Silicki is passionate about her customers. She notes, "We created customer relationships not because they drove loyalty and repeat business, but rather because it simply felt right." As a result, lil omm built more than a studio – it built a tribe of clients that power the small business beyond its bricks and mortar location, which closed in early 2016.

Customer love lies at the heart of the lil omm brand. But being scripted has never been a part of the formula. With a team of nearly 50 contractors and employees at its peak, lil omm was built on listening, caretaking and customer service – attributes that Pleasance notes weren't for marketing. They're simply who she is and what she wanted for her brand. But to her, lil omm is more than a small business – it's a community.

lil omm's clientele is predominantly women, but lil omm also boasts a consistent handful of men who are proud to call themselves part of the tribe. Pleasance recalls one male customer – a buttoned-up brain researcher at Georgetown University – who emailed the studio one day to let them know that he was involved in an accident and wasn't able to make it to class. She dropped by his house with balloons and get well soon cards from the teachers and fellow students. The customer was blown away and shared with her how yoga and the lil omm approach changed his life, moving him toward an honest openness with himself he was unable to reach previously. His professional life and public persona had held him back, but practicing yoga with lil omm pushed him to find new inner strength and personal identity.

This one-on-one, impromptu act of customer love is modus operandi for lil omm. When lil omm had its own studio, the business maintained a Caring Community committee of staff and volunteers who were dedicated to embracing both those challenged by and celebrating life events. The regular customer love was made possible by the simplest of business approaches – listening. Pleasance notes that she empowered, encouraged and expected the team to listen and to love. If a customer mentioned a life moment, the team took notice. Generosity and a "just say yes" attitude sat at the heart of the lil omm studio. Expired class passes were accepted from over-scheduled and busy customers. Free class and childcare passes were available to teachers to distribute to customers as acts of customer love. Special requests for classes or times were honored when possible. Pleasance notes that this approach was just easier and felt better.

Today, lil omm thrives through retreats, workshops, member/teacher events, and classes taught at other studio locations – a success made possible by devoted customers, a tribe built through customer love.

Customer Milestones

Small businesses are great at celebrating their own milestones, like offering deals and hosting events to celebrate the company's five-year anniversary. But what about a customer's milestones? When businesses are truly a part of their customers' lives, they not only know about, but also share in life's moments together. The good times and the lousy ones, the major events and more everyday achievements.

I hear of many financial services providers, like wealth managers and CPAs, who recognize a client's retirement. And I absolutely adore the Connecticut-based pediatric dentist who gives his patients the opportunity to choose a gift from his extra special toy chest when they stop sucking their thumbs. The gift incentivizes the behavior both the dentist and parents want for the child's dental health, and it deepens the connection between the dentist and child, making the dentist feel more approachable. Wins all around. Plus, the dentist's office shares photos of each child who earns their prize on its Facebook page, a practice that instills great pride in the young patients.

"

I've learned that people will forget what you said, people will forget what you did, but people will never forget how you made them feel.

- Maya Angelou

"Holidays"

Take a quick scroll through your social media feed of choice and you'll see there's always something to celebrate.

My kids were thrilled to celebrate Eat Ice Cream for Breakfast Day, and I'm always happy to oblige on Margarita Day. Lots of small businesses are great at using these offbeat "holidays" to create social media fodder or blog posts. But they also offer a fun way to engage with and love on your customers.

Since we only work with small businesses, National Small Business Month (May) is one of our faves. One year, we sent clients a box of fresh Crayola crayons with an accompanying note that encouraged them to draw their growth plan, dreams, or next great idea. And with a name like Popcorn & Ice Cream, we definitely have plenty of opportunities to connect and engage with clients. One year, we hosted a popcorn happy hour to celebrate National Popcorn Poppin' Month – yes, a real thing sponsored by the National Popcorn Association. There was no education and no sales pitch – just fun with customers, popcorn and beer.

As you look at these programs or those associated with real holidays (up next), remember the word of caution in chapter 11 on content marketing – consider how relevant the connection is to your business. Don't force something to fit.

HOLIDAYS & SEASONS

Small businesses are great at sending holiday cards, but going beyond Thanksgiving, Christmas and New Year's can offer far greater opportunity to stand out. While holiday greetings are wonderful, they're typically received along with stacks of others. It's hard to be memorable.

The baby boutique that sends its babies cards for their first three birthdays also sends out Mother's Day cards. This gesture is far more relevant for their customers, not to mention that it creates a great connection. Speaking of Mother's Day, as a mom, I can't help but take note of the restaurants that make brunch a bit more special for moms with a flower or free dessert. Small touches like that make a huge impact.

Flipping gears entirely, I love the educational consulting company that sends its teacher and administrator customers a back-to-school survival kit the first week of September each year. The kit is filled with gifts to invigorate and inspire as the new year school kicks off, like fresh pencils, a Starbucks gift card, tea bags, hand cream, relaxing bath salts and more. I've also seen a similar program from a law firm that gets many referrals from CPAs. Recognizing the value of these referral partners and stressful time of year, they deliver gift baskets during tax season with energy drinks, healthy snacks, junk food, and plenty of Advil.

THE BOTTOM LINE

Small businesses that take the time to love on their customers see the love returned to them. You don't have to love equally on all customers or break the bank doing so, but do keep in mind that your customers include everyone involved in getting your products and services to your end buyer. As you look for ways to love your customers, consider these general areas of opportunity:

- Service delivery

- Customer service

- Birthdays and anniversaries

- Customer milestones

- "Holidays"

- Holidays and Seasons

Chapter 15

Promoting Loyalty

Customer-oriented businesses build loyalty
each and every day. All of your communications
and engagement, your customer love, your
excellent service – they all support loyalty.
But there are also ways to be more intentional and
focused on increasing stickiness with customers.
Both customer loyalty programs and guarantees
directly contribute to building and nurturing
long-term customer relationships.

Loyalty Programs

Certainly customers enjoy and appreciate
incentives that encourage repeat purchases.
And customers are more likely to shop at a store
or from a vendor that offers a loyalty program,
particularly if you sell something commoditized.

But beyond rewarding customers, loyalty
programs offer the opportunity to get to know your
customers' habits, preferences and motivations.
With the data you collect from those enrolled
in your loyalty program, you are empowered to
evaluate product and marketing campaign

performance in customer-centered ways. You can look at age, gender, zip code, and numerous other categories to determine what resonates and drives customer behavior based on real numbers, not anecdotal feedback or more general financial analysis.

In addition, customer loyalty programs give you a direct opportunity to secure more personal customer preferences and details – information you can use to personalize and tailor your communications and customer love programs. So as you build your program, consider what customer data points would be most valuable to your business. Beyond the basic contact details and demographics, these pieces of information may include communications preferences, birthdays, colleges attended, hobbies and interests. You don't necessarily have to collect all of the information up front. Depending on the system or tools you use to manage the program, you can gather additional details via your communications plan or engagement strategy. For example, you could piggyback on the NCAA Tournament and use it as a hook to ask participating customers to visit their online profiles and add their college information.

I mentioned systems and tools – many exist that make managing customer loyalty programs easier for you and improve the participation experience for your customers. To evaluate which is best for your business, first frame your loyalty program. As the goal for a loyalty program is to encourage participation and reward repeat purchase, make sure that your business' priorities are integrated into the structure of the program. Consider...

What Behaviors Do You Want to Recognize?

Reward both the behaviors you want to encourage and the most common ways customers connect with your business.

How Will You Reward Participation?

I'm a big fan of tiered levels and rewards – they help make the value of the program quickly evident to newly enrolled customers and provide continuing rewards for those who have participated for some time. In addition, regular rewards keep customers coming back more frequently. Ensure that the rewards you select offer real value without an additional purchase commitment from the customer. In other words, don't offer $5 off a purchase of $25 or more as a reward. Simply give customers $5 to spend however they like, no matter how large or small the purchase to which they apply their earned benefit.

How Will You Drive Participation and Ongoing Engagement?

Make sure that you outline a communications plan that promotes the loyalty program and reminds customers about it on an ongoing basis.

Looking beyond rewards, loyalty programs also offer a great opportunity to engage with a select group of customers and show them some group customer love. You'll drive greater engagement in the program and a stronger connection with your business by making participants feel special via exclusive discounts, early access to new products or members-only events.

GUARANTEES & WARRANTIES

When you stand behind your product or service, customers are far more likely to have faith in your offerings, too. Guarantees and warranties demonstrate your confidence in the quality of your offering, willingness to stand behind the product you deliver and honesty of the marketing promises you make. A warranty also gives your customers confidence that they made a good purchasing decision when choosing you. Customer confidence is a strong contributor to customer loyalty.

Standing behind your products and services doesn't require a formal loyalty program. Delivering as promised and making situations right when unforeseen issues occur demonstrates a commitment to quality. However, if a more formal warranty makes sense for your business, here are some key things to look at when defining your program.

Satisfaction or Functionality?

Consider whether your warranty is a satisfaction guarantee or simply a commitment to functionality of the product. If a product doesn't meet a customer's needs but performs as stated, are you willing to take it back for a refund? Be clear in messaging as to the specifics of the program so customers know what's covered and what's not.

Make it Easy!

Yes – this is one of the rules of being customer-centric. Don't make it hard for customers to take you up on your warranty. If they say it doesn't work, then it doesn't work. Don't make them go to excruciating lengths to prove it. You'll erase every ounce of trust, confidence, and, along with it, customer satisfaction.

Set a Reasonable Timeframe For Your Warranty.

If a product's reasonable life is only a year, don't warranty it for three. Aside from keeping replacement levels within reason, it will help set the customer's expectation for the likely lifetime of the product. And please, if someone calls with a claim on day 366 of a one-year warranty program, honor the concern and request. You'll gain a loyal customer.

Implement Systems For Execution.
Consider how customers will prove date of purchase, how the claims process will work, and how you'll replace the product. Then clearly communicate these details on product packaging, on your website and to product resellers/retailers.

The Bottom Line

With a customer-centric approach, your business is building loyalty each and every day – with every interaction, engagement and act of customer love. But the opportunity exists to amplify the stickiness of customer relationships with more formalized programs.

Customer loyalty programs that reward customers for frequent or recurring purchases, store visits or referrals all strongly encourage customers to return time and again. Building on a different driver of loyalty – customer confidence – product warranties and service guarantees can also directly contribute to supporting long-term customer relationships.

Regardless of the path you take to building customer loyalty for your business, take the time to define a program that is easy for customers to engage with. Overcomplicating participation can quickly lead to frustration or anger, the opposite of the confidence the program was intended to build.

Section 3

GETTING BEYOND YOUR LIST

Chapter 16

Getting Beyond Your List

Section three, chapter 16, page 139, we finally get to "marketing!" Yes, of course this entire book is about marketing. But now we dive into the tactics that most business owners more typically associate with marketing – the outbound efforts focused on reaching new audiences.

At this point, you've established a super customer-friendly business. You're actively engaging with your customers. You're showering them with love and they're buying more and more. You're making a memorable impact, and referrals are rolling in naturally. Awesome! But...

In the last section, we talked about the risks of forsaking the customers you already have in favor of constantly reaching new ones. We went through the many benefits of – and lots of different ideas for – creating customer engagement and love. But, at the same time, constantly hitting the same folks over and over won't provide long-term growth. Depending on your business, your existing customers may have bought all they can from you. Or maybe they've outgrown your offering. Or perhaps you've done a great job of nurturing the leads in your pipeline (more on that in this chapter, too) and you need new names. Your low-hanging fruit is picked and gone. So just as investing in customer engagement is critical, so, too, is getting beyond your list.

In this section, we'll conquer a few of the many promotional channels and tactics that can help your small business reach new customers. Yes, many new customers can come from referrals, but relying solely on word of mouth is the same as focusing only on the customers you already have – after all, referrals come from existing customers.

Whether you have an established business, just launched the most awesome product ever, opened the hottest new spot in town, or expanded to offer a life-changing service, if no one knows about it, can you really be awesome, hot, or life-changing? No. You need to shout from the rooftops and share the news with not only your existing customers, but also your neighbors, friends, and those who don't yet know you. Some days you'll shout louder than others, but maintaining a constant drumbeat at some level is essential.

All too often, I hear new business owners or aspiring entrepreneurs talk about holes in the market and that if they launch a product, sales will come. They channel their inner *Field of Dreams* fan, thinking the "If you build it, they will come" concept will work. Unfortunately, it won't. Much as we'd love for famous ballplayers to simply come out of the cornfields to draw attention to our businesses, this isn't Iowa via Hollywood. Even if you do hail from the Hawkeye State, prospective customers need to know (and be reminded again and again) that you exist, and they need a compelling reason to come back for more. Even in the age of social media and Buzzfeed, simply standing up a website isn't enough.

Glen's Garden Market:
Making Change, One Bite at a Time

Just two weeks before Glen's Garden Market, a neighborhood grocery, was set to open its doors in the Dupont Circle area of Washington DC, the management team sat down to review the many marketing activities planned for grand opening weekend and beyond. One team owner raised a concern – "Why are we doing all of this? The neighbors know we're opening and they're psyched. The community is buzzing. We're going to have incredible food that people want. Seems like we're spending an awful lot of time and money when it isn't even necessary. The buzz is enough."

The question stopped the business owner, Danielle, in her tracks. A third-generation entrepreneur, Danielle knows what it takes to be successful. She quickly explained why buzz wasn't enough to keep the register ringing (or swiping, in today's day and age). And then she continued to review the public relations, special events, advertising, social media, direct mail, in-store and other marketing programs that were planned.

The grand opening proved a great success, with more than 1,100 customers shopping on opening day alone. In addition, Glen's Garden Market garnered 60 media stories, including many features, all of which contributed to consistent foot traffic after the initial marketing push.

Since opening, Glen's Garden Market has continued outbound marketing efforts to grow the store's audience, including positioning both the store and Danielle as thought leaders in the local food movement. This effort is responsible for Danielle's invitation to give a TEDx talk and serve as a judge of the Good Food

Awards. The store enjoys continued media coverage, including regular placements in *The Washington Post.*

Notably, Glen's Garden Market works closely with the local food artisans and startup businesses whose products fill the store's shelves, and it has embraced a collaborative approach to marketing. Danielle and her team consider the small, growing businesses that they buy from as partners more than vendors. As a result, as of April 2016, Glen's Garden Market has helped to launch more than 50 new products – giving start-up food companies an audience (the store's shoppers) and providing customers with new and innovative products nearly every week. With the store's ongoing commitment to helping other food artisans succeed, the number grows every month. On the flip side, the more established brands that Glen's buys from have lent their voices to help grow the Glen's audience – hosting seasonal launches in the store and actively engaging on social media.

Beyond truly getting the need to reach new audiences, Danielle lives and breathes customer engagement and customer service. It's part of her DNA. Just two months before opening, in the throes of store construction and product selection, she took her management team to meet with the team at Mitchells, a department store in Greenwich, Connecticut. Mitchells has literally written the book on customer love (more on this incredible resource at hugyourcustomers.com and in the "Thank You. Thank You." wrap-up at the conclusion of the book). This store provides both inspiration and lessons from which any small business can learn. I was honored to join the team on this visit. Danielle then took the team on a tour of a few of the top food establishments in New York to learn from the best.

With customer commitment starting at the top, customer engagement and customer service lie at the heart of the Glen's Garden Market brand. The store values customer feedback and uses it to help guide the business. Feedback has led to the introduction of new products on the store's shelves, an expanded menu of house-made prepared foods, and innovative community engagement programs.

Building on the success of the first store, Danielle opened the doors on a second location in December 2015. While less than 2 miles away from its first store, the new location in the hot Shaw neighborhood draws an entirely different clientele. Glen's is already listening to their new customers and evolving to meet their needs.

THE BOTTOM LINE

While nurturing your existing customer base is essential, so, too, is connecting with new audiences. To expand your reach to an ever-increasing pool of prospective customers, take stock of the many marketing opportunities available. As you evaluate each, apply your now-refined customer-centric lens. Not every approach will make sense for your business, and not every platform will resonate with your customers. Plus, many are expensive. So revisit your goals, your brand's vision, and your customer profile. Which of the many marketing opportunities are most appropriate and valuable for your business? Choose those that offer the greatest anticipated return for your marketing investment.

CHAPTER 17
GIVE IT AWAY

A couple of years ago, I got a call from an eager entrepreneur who was working on marketing plans for her soon-to-open gourmet popcorn shop. Considering the name of my company (Popcorn & Ice Cream), I thought there couldn't possibly be a more perfect client! Boy, was I wrong.

The woman on the other end of the line told me about her plans for her new artisan popcorn shop. She was opening a bricks and mortar location in a busy retail area that served an upper-middle class community with tons of young families. She planned to sell out of the storefront, but use the majority of the square footage in this pricey neighborhood for production and distribution through her other sales channels – wholesale customers and a monthly subscription service. Love it!

But then our conversation started to break down. She wasn't calling to discuss ideas for marketing this exciting and tasty new business. Rather, she was looking for recommendations for promotional products companies. Specifically, she wanted to know if I knew of a good vendor for magnets. I was confused. Magnets? She explained that she wanted to get the word out about the new business by participating in the many neighborhood events that bring the community together – and bring them literally to her store's doorstep. She would give attendees at the spring fair, summer picnic, fall festival and other events a magnet to promote the store, and she would sell popcorn from her booth. She believed that by giving potential customers a magnet, they'd remember her store name and have her phone number and website right at their fingertips. While I loved the approach to participation in the events, the magnets? Not so much.

It's not that branded promotional products don't have value – they do. But in this case, they didn't make sense as the primary giveaway. (As an aside, I don't love magnets as they're heavy to carry to events and many people now have stainless steel appliances to which magnets won't stick. But I digress.) In this case, my concern with the approach was that the business owner was overlooking the lowest cost and most impactful giveaway – her product! I suggested she give away popcorn samples to allow attendees at the event to get a taste of what they'd buy. Considering she had many unique flavors, this approach would allow her to show off her delicious popcorn and quickly convince people to buy.

The business owner refused. She felt that if she gave folks a taste, they wouldn't have any incentive to buy. Assuming the product was fabulous, I couldn't disagree more. In fact, she'd be removing the "will I like it?" barrier and encourage purchases. Needless to say, we didn't work together.

The lesson from this story applies whether you're selling popcorn or professional services: People are more likely to buy once they've tried a sample. I'd never suggest undercharging or giving every customer ongoing freebies. But going beyond a product or service description to providing customers with a taste of your product, expertise or working style, you give them a chance to experience you and your offering. When you give it away, you instantly move beyond "I'm worth it because I said so" to allowing customers to truly understand why you're worth the investment – no matter how large or small.

How this plays out depends on your business. For food and beverage products, the giveaway is obvious – whether at a community festival or in a retail shop, samples are easy and inexpensive. A little taste will certainly whet many buyers' appetites. Likewise, a "first class free" offer from a boutique fitness studio can get a new athlete hooked without additional out-of-pocket costs – the teacher is already there and likely not compensated based on the number of participants in a class.

Samples from professional service providers don't have to be complicated either. Consider a free 30-minute call that allows you to showcase your smarts and your perspective. Sure, you could be billing someone else for the time, but the half hour of time is an investment in future revenue. If you're not comfortable giving away your time, consider content – whitepapers, ebooks, video tutorials, or blog posts – to give your prospects an opportunity to understand how you think and the value you provide.

"

When you give it away, you instantly move beyond "I'm worth it because I said so" to allowing customers to truly understand why you're worth the investment – no matter how large or small.

One quick note on using content as your sample/giveaway. Give some content away without strings, like your blog. Should you choose to gate your content – requiring interested readers to provide their name and email address to access the material – recognize that this is a lead generation strategy, not a giveaway. This too is a great approach. But if you do go down this road, be sure the content provides real value that the prospect feels is worth handing over their contact information for. And, follow up on those leads! After all, that's why you asked for someone's information in the first place – not just to dump them on your email newsletter list.

When it comes to retail, giving it away can be trickier, but by no means impossible. You can partner with your vendors to offer giveaways or host contests that incentivize new customers to come into the store. Once they're there, make sure they have the experience they'll come to appreciate as a regular customer.

Get creative! The idea is to provide the opportunity to experience YOU. How that looks is different for every business.

THE BOTTOM LINE

Why does your target market buy from you? They don't buy because you say so in your marketing materials. They don't buy because of the awards on the wall or because someone else said you're great (though awards are awesome, too – more on borrowed credibility in chapter 20). Your target market buys from you because they have a clear understanding of your value and excellence. When you offer a sample, you give potential customers the opportunity experience what makes you fabulous, and you move them more quickly towards a purchase.

CHAPTER 18

THE POWER
OF NETWORKING

When my husband first started out in the financial services industry, he came home one night from training with the concept of "ABC" – Always Be Closing – stuck in his head. The sales meeting that day was focused on both how to grow your pipeline of new leads and how to move the leads through the pipeline to close sales and grow your client base, a concept made popular by the 1992 movie *Glengarry Glen Ross*. This made me cringe – so salesy, especially for something as emotional as personal finances. But while I hate the way the idea was taught to a room of freshly minted financial advisors, I do agree with the heart of the message.

As a small business owner, no matter how many sales associates or business development resources you have in place, you're responsible for building your business. Making new connections and building relationships is critical for continued growth and reaching new customers. I always tell clients, "You never know who knows who. You never know where your next great opportunity to grow will come from." So, while I don't think you always need to be "closing," as a small business owner, you do need to be constantly networking to build your business.

Networking is all about selling yourself. After all, if you don't, no one else can for you. However, it doesn't mean you're always at the ready with an "I can do that" or "Stop by the store – we'll take care of you" when reading messages on your neighborhood listserv or picking up your kids at school. Networking doesn't have to feel awkward or pushy, like the forced lead sharing that is all too common in some business development groups. But effective networking does go beyond simply swapping business cards.

When it comes to small business networking, it is about making new connections through those you already know or those you should know. Networking is about building relationships and empowering others to be an advocate for your business. And networking is as much about listening as it is about talking. Being an active listener allows you to pick up on opportunities to connect and provide value, as well as to offer ideas of how you can help someone to meet their goals or overcome challenges.

To reach new customers, you need to be where your customers are. You need to connect with them through networks they're a part of and in ways that they trust. Networking allows you to place your business at the center of these networks and reach new customers through those they already know.

YOUR EXISTING NETWORK

One of the easiest ways to connect with new customers is also the most often overlooked by new small business owners – through people you already know! However, small business owners tend to fall into one of two categories when it comes to reaching those within their networks – the over-sharer or the under-seller.

The Over-Sharer

We all have "that friend" on Facebook who posts seemingly nonstop about his or her business. These are often friends involved in multi-level marketing businesses such as health shakes and jewelry. You don't want to be that girl or guy.

The Under-Seller

On the flip side, many small business owners mistakenly assume that their friends are not interested. This is rarely the case! While a friend or family member may not be in your target market, they want to know what you're up to and have the opportunity to support you. Plus, you never know who knows who – remember this chapter is all about making new connections!

"

Networking is about building relationships and empowering others to be an advocate for your business.

The goal is not to guilt everyone you know into becoming a customer but rather to empower your network to help you increase your reach. You want to make sure that your network is aware of what you do and who your ideal customer is. It is possible that they're a potential customer or partner themselves. In many cases, however, someone you know knows an ideal customer or partner for you or can make a connection toward one.

While I'd never encourage you to bulk add everyone in your personal address book to your business email list, if you're launching a new business, don't be afraid to shout it from the rooftops! Send an email or even two to your network. Give them the chance to refer you to others they know or give you a shout out on a listserv or social media. Yes, you can absolutely ask for shout outs! You can also offer your network suggestions on what to say. Again – don't be pushy, but also don't be afraid to ask. Let friends, family and others in your existing network be part of your journey toward greatness.

If you're on the shyer side, consider a personal Facebook announcement in lieu of an email. Facebook is also a great place to share news about a new product line or big annual sale. Use your discretion and share only the most noteworthy information. For folks who want to know more, encourage them to like your business page, connect through other social media channels, or subscribe to your email list.

"
To reach new customers, you need to be where your customers are. You need to connect with them through networks they're a part of and in ways that they trust.

INDUSTRY ASSOCIATIONS, CHAMBERS OF COMMERCE & OTHER ORGANIZED GROUPS

Being where your customers are is essential when it comes to selecting which groups to participate in and affiliate with. There are an endless sea of networking groups and professional, special interest and local community organizations you can join. As a result, it's easy to fall into a trap of investing significant time or money in a group that yields little return despite promises of great connections. Be selective when you consider which organizations provide the greatest value for your specific goals, and only join as many as you can truly make the most of.

No matter the group(s) you choose, take the time to engage. Simply signing up and paying membership dues will not pay dividends in growing your business. You get out what you put in, so go to meetings and events, read and (if possible) contribute to the newsletter, and consider sponsorship and advertising when it makes sense. (There's more on pay-for-play opportunities in chapter 21.)

Engagement requires an investment of time to build relationships with others in the room. I often hear small business owners gripe that they're not getting good leads through their networking efforts. Most often, it turns out that their expectations are unrealistic, and they're not taking the time to build relationships. As I mentioned at the beginning of this chapter, simply swapping business cards offers little value. Neither you nor the individual behind the piece of fancy tiny paper in your hand know enough to make valuable connections for the other.

The objective of networking is building relationships – not collecting business cards or making sales pitches. To build relationships that will result in value for both you and the person you've met, ask questions beyond "what do you do?" and listen to the answers. What does your brand stand for? What's your approach to business? Who's your ideal customer? By listening first, you can contribute information about your business that's valuable and relevant to those you're connecting with. And you can avoid an icky sales pitch. With strong relationships, the opportunities for referrals and sales come naturally.

Also remember that professional networking is a two-way street. Others are networking with you to build their businesses as much as you're connecting with them to build yours. Give as much as you get. Or give more. And if your generosity goes unreciprocated or underappreciated, reevaluate the relationship. In this case, you're likely connected with the wrong individual. It's time to build new relationships with others who share your customer-centric passion.

> **"**
> **The objective of networking is building relationships – not collecting business cards or making sales pitches.**

How to Choose Which Groups to Join

Every industry has a professional association. These organizations are incredibly valuable for staying on top of the latest trends and products, seeing what the competition is up to, getting great new ideas, and recruiting new employees. But they rarely drive customers directly. While affiliation with the association can give you credibility as an expert in your industry, you will spend your time networking and connecting with the competition. Instead, consider where your customers are and where others who target the same audience hang out.

For B2B (business to business) businesses, ask yourself which industries you target. Who is your buyer? For example, in a previous life, I worked for a marketing agency whose client roster was filled with technology companies, most of whom were government contractors. We were active members of the Armed Forces Communications & Electronics Association (AFCEA), an organization whose membership was comprised of both military technology leaders and the civilian government contractors that served them. Participation in this group provided us with highly valuable networking opportunities with our clients, prospective clients, and the agencies they served. By being present, we demonstrated our commitment to their work and also stayed on top of the issues of importance and interest to them.

For B2C (business to consumer) businesses, your organizational involvement likely will go beyond industry associations to organizations that support your customers' specific needs or interests. And don't overlook the power of influencers! Oftentimes the best path to your customers is through other complementary products or service providers in an industry. For example, when an organic sports drink launched, it focused on engaging with personal trainers. As a result, their reach was multiplied with every potential customer that the trainers worked with at the gym. (You'll find more on influencer marketing in chapter 20.)

No matter your business type, don't forget to go local! Every small business operates at a local level – whether you have a pizza joint on the corner of Main Street, sell your widget online or offer professional services to customers across the country. Your local business community can be a powerful ally in growing your business. Chambers of commerce, your local Rotary and the many, many local chapters of networking groups can be excellent sources of connection to the community in which you operate. These groups are often rich in partnership and referral opportunities. You will meet other small business owners who understand the value of relationships and also have large networks. By sharing your customer-centric focus, you will give fellow members confidence that you'll deliver top service to anyone they refer to you.

Beyond these groups, there are a growing number of both general and specialized business development organizations. These provide fantastic opportunities to meet other small business owners facing similar challenges and work together to grow everyone's businesses. However, these should not be looked to for marketing and networking purposes, as that is not their intent.

LINKEDIN

LinkedIn is Facebook for business. No matter your industry or business, LinkedIn can be a valuable source of new customers. The platform allows you to sell yourself to prospective customers before they even pick up the phone or walk through your door. While your website provides one level of information online, your LinkedIn profile offers a different view into your background and persona. Your connections and recommendations build credibility, trust, and a level of comfort. If a connection sees that people they trust and admire have worked with you, they are far more likely to work with you as well.

And beyond providing prospective customers or partners with a sense for your qualifications, it allows you to check them out in advance, too. To make the most of your LinkedIn experience, follow these tips.

Build Your Profile

What aspects of your background are most important to potential customers and most relevant to the business you own today? Focus on these, making sure that your tone of voice mirrors that of your small business brand – the one you created with your customer in mind. Like your business, your LinkedIn profile must speak to your brand. Take the time to complete as many sections as you can with relevant details, including awards you've won, volunteer positions you've held and publications you've, well, published. And while you want to focus on your current business, don't skip the other areas of your professional journey – they all led you to this point.

Connect

Connections are the foundation of networking. Beyond connecting with everyone you've worked with, connect with personal contacts as well. As I mentioned at the beginning of this chapter, give your friends and family the opportunity to support you and your business by engaging in this low-commitment way. Each time you meet someone new, connect on LinkedIn.

Connections allow prospects to see who else you know and who you have in common, empowering them to ask those individuals for feedback or an endorsement. And connections allow you to be found by the connections of your connections – giving you credibility by way of association.

Content

LinkedIn provides you with the opportunity to build thought leadership. Publish articles that allow you to engage in meaningful conversations with customers and others in your industry. This is a great way to extend the life and reach of your blog posts.

Get Smart

Just as prospective customers and partners can learn more about you from your LinkedIn profile, you can get smart about them as well. This is particularly valuable for B2B businesses and partner relationships. Read up on those you're going to meet or wanting to do business with. LinkedIn can give you insights on their experience, interests, education, volunteer work and more. Plus, if they've published posts, you can learn more about their perspective and use all of this information to make for more engaging conversations.

Perhaps the most valuable information you can glean from a prospect's LinkedIn profile, however, is through their connections. Do you know anyone in common? If so, you can ask for an introduction to a prospect you'd like to meet or additional insights from one you're already engaged with.

THE BOTTOM LINE

As with every recommendation in this book, adapt your networking strategy to your business, your target customers, and, in this case, your personal comfort level and personality. Introvert or extrovert, there's a networking strategy that can be impactful for your small business.

Networking can take many forms. Regardless of the path, it offers an invaluable way to reach new customers through those you already know or groups with which you associate. As you evaluate networking opportunities, remember:

- Listen first. Ask questions to understand someone's situation and needs, then provide relevant information that is specific to them; avoid a blanket sales pitch.

- Sell yourself! If you don't, no one else will.

- Effective networking takes more than swapping cards – take the time to build real relationships.

- Start networking with those you already know!

- Be where your customers are.

Chapter 19

Partnerships & Collaboration

When your business is awesome, you'll have the opportunity to partner with many other businesses for marketing. And it's no wonder they'll want in on your fabulousness – your customers love you, you have high levels of customer engagement, your brand is admired, and your business is on a noteworthy path upward.

Plus, once you've mastered your networking strategy, you'll undoubtedly have met many other amazing small business owners you'll want to work with. It will be tempting to join forces and market to one another's customers; partner marketing can have immense benefits and provide great opportunities to reach new customers. (Before we go further, I want to clarify that by "partner" I mean work with another business for marketing, not form a legal or financial partnership.)

Small business owners are often quick to interview other small business owners as guest bloggers or offer one another's customers 10% off. While not bad ideas in theory, the approaches rarely drive new business in practice. Why? They're opportunistic and fail to consider the value to either business's customers. As a result, they draw precious time and resources away from more valuable marketing or customer engagement efforts.

Before spamming your customers with coupons and offers from a new business bestie, consider whether the relationship makes sense. Begin with the end in mind – what is your goal for the collaboration? Will the marketing effort you and the potential partner are discussing help you meet your goals?

Start by confirming that your business values align. If your focus is on service and the other business's focus is on speed, there may be a mismatch. Your customers will expect the same service and approach from the partner business as they do from you. Also, if you aren't already familiar with the other business, do your homework. Confirm that the business has strong online reviews and happy customers. By associating with the other business, you align your brand with theirs. If they fall short of your customer's expectations, those shortcomings reflect on your business, too. Finally, ensure there's customer overlap. While you both may target the same broad category, the specifics of your customer sets may not align.

Once you've confirmed that your brands align, focus conversations with the potential partner on each business and, importantly, each set of customers. As you define your collaboration, consider:

What's In It For You?

What does your business stand to gain by partnering with this other business? What do they bring to the table? Does the alliance help you reach new audiences? Or can you draw valuable borrowed equity from being associated with this other business or entrepreneur? There's more on borrowed equity in the next chapter.

What's In It For Them?

The same questions that apply to you also apply to the other business. What does the other business stand to gain by aligning with yours? What's your give?

What's In It For Both of Your Customers?

Beyond benefits to your respective businesses, consider the value to both your customers and theirs. Do your customers want discounts to the other business? Or does the partner offer a unique perspective, complementary resources, or valuable services your customers can benefit from?

Once you've determined that a collaborative marketing effort makes sense and provides great value to both your and your partner's customers, it's time to share the news. Like every marketing program, if no one knows about it, it can't meet your goals. So share the mutual love – tell others about the alliance and how everyone wins.

One caveat – respect your customers and their relationship with you. If your customers haven't consented to receiving marketing messages from other businesses and you suddenly start sending regular dedicated emails promoting your partners, they'll quickly get cranky – no matter how valuable the offers. So consider the best way to deliver a partner discount and communicate the benefits of the relationship.

IDENTIFYING PARTNERS

Partner marketing isn't limited to those you already know. If you offer a valuable add-on to another product or service, go after the partners you want! Flip back to chapter 18 on networking, but really hone your efforts to reach and connect with a specific target in mind – either a category or a company – that meets the above criteria (shared brand values, customer alignment, benefits to both you and the partner, and, of course, benefits to the customers).

One area of potential partner marketing opportunity that is often overlooked is those in your sales chain. If you're a product company, explore opportunities to collaborate on outreach and marketing with your distributors or retailers (and vice versa). Working together amplifies sales for everyone and underscores your commitment to one another's success. Plus, when you share the costs of a marketing program, your individual marketing spend decreases and your reach increases.

Remember the story of Glen's Garden Market (chapter 16)? I love their approach to partner marketing. The store is committed to introducing new products to its customers, thus providing a launch pad for artisan food brands that share its local, natural focus. Glen's actively promotes the brands it carries via in-store sampling and other events. The food brands gain immediate credibility through association with Glen's and an audience of prospective buyers. In return, the products actively promote their presence on Glen's shelves and drive buyers to the store.

Beyond the social media shoutouts (of which there are many), Glen's Garden Market often collaborates with the brands on its shelves, in its refrigerator cases, and on tap to offer unique customer programming – squarely delivering value for the store, the product companies and customers. For example, Glen's hosts release parties that give its customers the opportunity to experience new and seasonal flavors offered by its partner product companies. This generates news for its partners, who generate sales. Glen's owner, Danielle, is so committed to promoting brands the store helped launch that she dedicated the store's third birthday party to the "Women of the Watershed" – the 25 entrepreneurs whose businesses have thrived as a result of their initial collaborations.

The Bottom Line

Partner marketing and collaboration can be highly valuable to reach new customers for both participating businesses. While it can be tempting to partner with a friend's business just because there's a personal relationship, without a planned approach, the value is limited. Instead, consider aligning with other small businesses where there is good brand and customer compatibility. It's ok to seek these out!

To make the most of the time and financial resources you commit to the relationship, take care to evaluate the partner and define goals for the relationship. Ask yourself:

- Do we share common business values?

- Do we share a common target market?

- Does this business have happy customers and a good reputation?

- What's in it for me?

- What's in it for them?

- What's in it for our customers?

CHAPTER 20

BORROWING EQUITY

"We need press."

Small business owners love to love the media. What's not to love? Press coverage can extend your reach to new audiences by hundreds, thousands, or millions of eyeballs at a time. Online articles and backlinks from publications can drive traffic to your website, boost search ranking, and make you more visible. However, one of the biggest benefits press coverage provides is increased credibility of your business in your customers' eyes.

Press coverage works in the same way as a referral or positive online review – providing prospects with confidence that others value your perspective, your products and your business. It allows you to get beyond your own claims of being fantastic and lets others do the talking for you. And it also allows you to borrow brand equity from the news outlet in which you appear. By being associated with a respected broadcast station, or print or online publication, your business earns credibility by association.

Media relations is often referred to as public relations, or PR. These terms are just the means to the end – reporter relationships. Getting the media to take notice isn't always easy, and establishing a rapport with reporters requires ongoing care and attention. If you're pursuing a PR strategy, consider the reporters you target as another customer.

Just like customers, reporters are bombarded with thousands of messages every day. They need a reason to care, so you need to help them understand why your perspective is relevant to their audience. The fact is, news is a product, too, and reporters have customers to keep engaged.

As you consider how you engage members of the media, consider your customers. What stories or topics are interesting to your customers? What's happening in the world or in your customers' lives that makes your business relevant to them? Focus your pitches on these areas rather than pushy product messages. Position your products, services and expertise around concepts and ideas that are relevant to your customers and reporters' audiences. Even company news must be anchored in a "why" message – pitches that read like a brochure are certain to be ignored.

As you look at where to take your message, go back to your customers. What publications do they read? Where do they seek information about your type of product or service? Start there. While large national media outlets provide expansive reach, trade and lifestyle publications, as well as smaller local networks, can often help you connect with an audience more in line with your customers. And don't forget about online publications and bloggers. These more modern media properties can be valuable, influential and help you reach highly targeted audiences.

When you secure the almighty press hit, make the most of it! When the article runs or video clip airs, the audience you reach often drives increased web traffic, social media follows, and sometimes sales. But the real benefit of the media coverage is just beginning. Think of the power of the "as seen in" string of logos on a website – immediate credibility. And how good will your customers feel about their purchases from you when they learn that a reputable media outlet also took notice?

Borrowing equity from others to grow your business doesn't have to be limited to the press, however. Public relations is only one of many paths that affords a small business the opportunity to increase relevance and reputation by way of others.

> **"**
>
> Awards reinforce and highlight what customers already know – that you're noteworthy. Awards tell prospects that an authority recognizes your value and quality – and that they're willing to stand behind you, give you their seal of approval, and lend their brand equity to you.

AWARDS

If you're a new business, awards offer immediate credibility. And if you're more established, awards reinforce and highlight what customers already know – that you're noteworthy. Awards tell prospects that an authority recognizes your value and quality – and that they're willing to stand behind you, give you their seal of approval, and lend their brand equity to you.

Before Meghan Khaitan of MyBuckleMate sold a single unit, she applied for and earned a silver medal in the National Parenting Publications Awards program and the Mr. Dad Seal of Approval. Her product makes backseat seatbelt buckling easier for kids and those with limited mobility, addressing a frequent frustration. But while unique, Meghan was launching in the crowded children's products market and knew she would face challenges standing out. The awards gave her recognition and credibility that opened doors with early retail partners and customers. She was able to sell into an "award winning children's products" event on zulily, an online flash sale retailer with which Meghan has since enjoyed a long-standing wholesale relationship that has driven tens of thousands of sales.

SPEAKING GIGS

Want to be seen as an authority in your industry? Get behind the podium – or out in front if that's more your presentation style. Speaking opportunities empower you to build name recognition and become a thought leader on topics relevant to your business. As a result, you drive greater awareness for your business and reach new audiences you don't have to find or work to create. When you speak at a conference, the organizers fill the room. They promote the overall event, including your remarks. You reach the individuals they spend time and money to assemble. Beyond the reach, you again earn that borrowed credibility by being associated with the event. The added win is potentially connecting with reporters, as they often cover noteworthy events.

One caveat – speaking opportunities range from instances where you are paid for your participation to ones where you have to ante up some cash to say a few words and many "free" variations in between. How do you decide if an opportunity is worth your investment of time or money? Consider the number of attendees, name recognition of the event, potential reach, ability to secure attendee names and contact information, likelihood of press attendance and any number of other criteria that help you meet your business goals. (For more details on choosing where and how to invest, skip ahead to chapter 23.)

INFLUENCER MARKETING

Did you hear about the independent designer whose website crashed after Duchess Kate Middleton wore her dress to a public event? Talk about borrowed equity! While every small business can't land an unexpected, implied endorsement from a Queen-in-Waiting, numerous opportunities exist to reach your target customers through influencers, AKA, people whose opinions matter.

The notion of influencer marketing is trendy and evolving, especially because social media allows everyday individuals with an interest or passion to build a significant following. As you evaluate the influencers with whom you want to align, consider not only someone's following, but also how likely your target customers are to value that individual's opinion. And keep in mind that someone doesn't have to be an A-list (or even B-list) celebrity to carry a level of authority in your customers' and prospects' minds. As a result, influencer marketing can take many forms and draw on other aspects of your overall marketing strategy, including:

PR

Often, popular bloggers can deliver "media" coverage and serve as an influencer through what they write and what they share on social media. As a blogger's following grows, however, their price may go up, too. While there are still niche bloggers that will happily take free product in exchange for a review, the numbers are dwindling.

Networking

Customers go to trusted sources for recommendations and referrals each and every day. As a result, other small business owners can serve as a conduit to customers, particularly for target customers that are more distributed or harder to reach. Nurturing these relationships through networking and events specifically for them can pay significant dividends.

For example, TechMoxie provides one-on-one coaching and small group classes on everyday technology for older adults. To reach their audience, they engage with retirement communities and social workers that support seniors – organizations and individuals their customers trust, seek information from, and engage with on a regular basis. To expand their reach and provide value to these influencers, TechMoxie is notably active in local networking groups. They offer free seminars for influencers' communities, and they also host occasional workshops or breakfasts on topics of interest to influencers. Networking, free samples, and custom events all directly impact the success of TechMoxie's influencer engagement.

THE BOTTOM LINE

Aligning your small business with other credible sources allows you to borrow brand equity and relevance from other entities, including media outlets, conferences, awards and certifications or influential individuals.

New audiences you reach through these channels offer significant value. The power of these associations is amplified when you put them front and center to build your own brand – on your website, in your social media and content marketing efforts, and on your packaging.

While borrowing equity isn't always free, the value can outweigh the expense. Your investment of time in nurturing reporter relationships or hiring a PR firm to pitch the media, paying entry fees for awards competitions, or compensating an Instagram influencer can afford you reach you wouldn't otherwise be able to achieve and long-lasting credibility by association.

CHAPTER 21

PAY FOR PLAY

Even if you've successfully bootstrapped your small business and bartered your way as a participant in great events, sometimes a crisp dollar (or a fistful of them) is necessary to reach the audiences you want. On the flip side, maybe you're having a record-breaking year or just received an infusion of cash? Lucky you! Regardless of your situation, paying to play is sometimes the only option – one that is often more viable than many small business owners realize.

I'm a big fan of investing cold hard cash in marketing to support specific goals and business initiatives. There are times in the lifecycle of a small business when it's simply necessary – particularly for bricks and mortar business openings or new product launches. And when you're looking to invest, there is certainly no shortage of opportunities on which you can spend your marketing budget. This is where your customer-centric lens comes into play. In this chapter, being customer-centric is all about making choices that help you reach and connect with your target customers... and avoid wasting those precious limited marketing dollars.

No small business has money to burn. So when I suggest that there's value in reaching into your wallet, I'm by no means saying you have to break the bank. The goal is investing where your dollars can have the greatest return. It's easy to get caught up in sales pitches filled with promises of reaching thousands of eyeballs. But marketing budgets can be quickly depleted and campaigns can prove ineffective if they're only focused on building awareness and not on actually reaching and engaging your target customers. Branding is important, for sure. But your campaign's success can quickly be limited if you overlook educating your prospects on what you have to offer, connecting with them in ways that demonstrate you understand their needs, and providing them with a compelling reason to engage. There's nothing worse than investing in a marketing endeavor that results in prospects that say, "Oh yeah, I heard about X company... what do they do again?" This outcome is sure to have lackluster impact on sales objectives.

You'll find much more in chapter 23 on choosing the right programs for your business. For now, let's focus on some specific considerations when it comes to pay-for-play opportunities.

ADVERTISING

More years ago than I care to admit, I majored in advertising as an undergrad at Syracuse University's S.I. Newhouse School of Public Communications. At the time, digital media was in its infancy, and we studied media planning separately from creative development. Times have changed. A lot. Advertising is no longer limited to magazines, newspapers, broadcast and outdoor. The notion of buying only on a cost per thousand basis is a thing of the past. And advertising as a stand-alone tactic has been replaced by integrated marketing campaigns. Good thing! The evolution of advertising significantly benefits small businesses on smaller budgets. Today's advertising is far more accessible and audience targeting is far more precise.

One thing that hasn't changed is advertising's promise of getting your business in front of thousands (or millions!) of new customers. There's truth to this. But being in front of new audiences is only half the battle.

"

> Marketing budgets can be quickly depleted and campaigns can prove ineffective if they're only focused on building awareness and not on actually reaching and engaging your target customers.

Get the Right Eyeballs

Increasingly, advertising is a technology game as it allows you to be hyper-focused on reaching your specific target audience. By taking advantage of the many options available to narrow the focus of your campaign, you can limit wasted impressions and stretch your dollars further to reach the audiences you want.

For example, Facebook allows you use your existing list to target an audience that mirrors your customers both in terms of demographics and interests. You can exclude existing customers or market only to them. And this is only scratching the surface of the incredible advertising technology available. Online and offline media companies alike have better data than ever on their audiences, and they can really help you focus your campaigns so they reach the right people. Take advantage of these resources!

Get in Front of Customers – Literally

It's easy to get caught up in the allure of social media advertising or Google AdWords. But if you're a bricks and mortar retailer or only serve a specific local community, traditional offline or in-person advertising can be more impactful.

For example, advertising on the side of bus shelters, placing signs at a busy intersection, or handing out coupons on a street corner can drive significant foot traffic, customer inquiries and first-time purchases. In chapter 18, I talked about the need to be where your customers are. The same idea applies here. Consider where your customers are on a daily basis and where they access information. Sometimes, being physically present makes all the difference.

Plus, there is so much more to advertising than display ads and promoted posts! And getting beyond awareness for its own sake allows for more interesting campaigns that can often deliver stronger results.

One campaign that stands out to me offered real value – or at least the chance for real value – to customers. A new coffee shop that wanted to get the word out and compete against the big chains invested in a co-branded giveaway with a popular, local blog. The coffee shop's target customer was squarely in line with the blog's readers. It skipped the traditional display and newsletter ads and instead spent its dollars on a custom program that included a sponsored post about the shop and the contest. And the campaign also included multiple social media posts to drive greater awareness about the contest.

To enter, contest participants were required to provide their email address. They earned additional contest entries by liking the coffee shop's Facebook page and following them on Instagram. The grand prize winner received a cup of coffee every day for three months – a prize valued at $250. Additional winners of smaller prizes were also chosen.

The outcome was noteworthy. This new coffee shop collected 1,800 email addresses for future marketing (permission was granted as part of the contest rules) and hundreds of new Facebook likes and Instagram follows. Most importantly, however, sales went up during the contest – locals wanted to taste what they might win.

Tradeshows, Community Events & Sponsorships

In the last chapter, I shared thoughts on the value of speaking opportunities. But events can provide significant value in front of the podium, too. Whether at an industry tradeshow, a community program, or your own custom event, in-person events give you the ability to truly connect with customers and prospects, shake their hands, hear their concerns, and see their reactions. While incredibly powerful, events can also be incredibly expensive. So choose wisely and make the most of your airtime with attendees.

"

The evolution of advertising significantly benefits small businesses on smaller budgets. Today's advertising is far more accessible and audience targeting is far more precise.

More Than Numbers

Look beyond the number of expected event attendees. Bigger isn't always better. A smaller audience of targeted prospects or satisfied customers can provide far greater opportunity for engagement than thousands of less qualified individuals.

Beyond who will be at an event, determine what marketing opportunities it provides. Will you have a means to capture contact information or get a copy of the attendee list? Can you put your marketing collateral directly into attendees' hands? Are there ways to pay for increased visibility? What opportunities do you have to connect with other participating businesses?

While you might be focused primarily on customers and prospects, don't overlook networking opportunities. Others in attendance are potentially great partners considering that they're likely targeting the same customers as you.

Details, Details, Details

All too often, small businesses get caught up in the details and worry about minutiae that rarely makes a difference to customers. Except when it comes to events. This is one area where the sometimes overwhelming nature of a big presence causes small businesses to overlook the little things.

Successful engagement is all about execution. If you're hosting your own event, look beyond where you have openings on your calendar and, when planning, consider the day of the week, time of day and specific date that will work best for the greatest number of target attendees. Then, consider the details that make the event easy to attend and enjoyable for participants.

For example, if your event is outdoors, remember to have a backup plan for weather – unexpected rain or hot sunshine. If the location you choose has little-to-no parking, provide information in advance on where to park or how to valet at the door. If customers arrive frustrated because they couldn't find a parking spot, your opportunity for a successful outcome is reduced.

These are just a few examples of the many little details that can make a big difference in the success of an event. Just as you've walked through your business from your customer's perspective, walk through their event experience to make sure you consider the little nuances that make a difference in how you show up.

The Bottom Line

Sometimes there's just no way around it – you have to pay to play. When you find your business in a situation where you want to connect with specific or larger audiences, it might be time to tap the marketing budget. Make the most of your investment, which means:

- Choose wisely. Focus on opportunities where you can reach the greatest number of customers and prospects while minimizing waste.

- Get creative with the materials you create or the opportunities you choose. Oftentimes when you look beyond the obvious, your advertisements or events have a greater impact.

- Focus on the details. There's nothing worse than committing funds and getting super excited about a marketing endeavor only to have it underperform because something small is overlooked. Think through the effort from your customer's perspective – how will they most likely engage with your advertisement or event?

- Don't be afraid to spend some cash. Sometimes it's the only way. When executed well, small expenditures can pay huge dividends.

CHAPTER 22

EMBRACE COMMUNITY

Whether you have a bricks and mortar storefront, run a home-based business, or manufacture and distribute products nationwide, you are tightly interwoven into the communities in which you operate – creating jobs (yes, even if it's just your own, it counts!), supporting the economy, and serving those who live, work and play in your neighborhood, no matter how wide-reaching it may be. You define what "community" means to your business – it may be those who live within a few zip codes, or it may include an international audience of customers who share a common passion or interest.

Just as you support your local economy, the community supports you as customers, partners and neighbors. By playing an active role, you reinforce your commitment to it and demonstrate your appreciation of it. You can't get more customer-centric than that, as your community is both your customer and your lifeline as a small business.

Being active in your community can take many forms. Your business can donate a gift certificate to an elementary school auction, give away products and services to those in need, or sponsor a Little League team. Your employees can volunteer once a month. You can serve on the board of a nonprofit. No matter what you do, you make a difference.

I'm a big believer in giving back, and I'd argue that these efforts are about more than being generous – it is your responsibility as a business owner and small business, but it's also good for business. Being active and visible supports business growth by connecting you on a deeper level with current and prospective customers. Whether you give locally or align your business with a social cause at a national or international level, you build goodwill with current customers and connect with new ones.

> **"**
> Just as you support your local economy, the community supports you as customers, partners and neighbors. By playing an active role, you reinforce your commitment to it and demonstrate your appreciation of it.

As you already well know, you can choose from a number of marketing options to engage your customers and grow your business. Likewise, you can choose from an infinite number of organizations and causes to support. You may be approached directly by organizations, but often, it will be your own customers that present your business with opportunities to participate. Don't be afraid to focus your giving programs. You can choose to support what feels right to you, resonates with your customers or aligns with your business. You decide on the best fit for your small business. I only encourage caution when it comes to associating your business with organizations whose work may be at odds with some of your customers' values, such as political groups or those on one side or the other of controversial societal issues.

If you choose to make corporate giving or philanthropy a component of your business, do so because it feels right to you. Embrace it! Share it. Incorporate it into your sales strategy, communications plans and customer engagement programs. While simply writing a check is highly valuable to support the financial needs of an organization, it is limited in terms of its benefits to your business and your customers – plus you're overlooking an important business benefit.

Engage Your Customers in the Program

Including your customers in your giving strategy offers the greatest value to the organizations and causes you support and allows you to reap the greatest business benefit. For example, you might host events that bring your business and community together to support an organization's operations or goals. Or you might launch a social media campaign that encourages customers to share how they give back. Or perhaps you'll run limited-time promotions during which you'll donate a percentage of all purchases to a cause. Any of these ideas benefit the community and your business while engaging your customers in the process.

One of my favorite collaborations was run by two local organizations – a new restaurant just opening its doors and an established, well-respected and well-known nonprofit that provides support for families of children in the hospital. To provide both the kitchen and front-of-the-house (waiters and hostesses) teams a chance to practice on actual customers, the restaurant offered its entire menu for free during its first open weekend. Instead of paying for their meals, customers were encouraged to make a donation to the nonprofit instead (and of course tip their servers).

While a soft opening is a common practice for many restaurants, these meals weren't promoted primarily to friends and family – the norm in these situations. Instead, the nonprofit did the bulk of the outreach to its substantial donor/supporter list and lent its well-respected brand to the restaurant, a relative unknown at the time. As a result of the collaboration, the restaurant gained exposure to a significantly wider audience than it could have on its own, earned media coverage for its generosity, and achieved its operational goals of refining its customer service. The nonprofit raised more than $8,000 to support its programming. Huge wins all around.

No matter the approach you take or programs you run as part of your giving strategy, communicate, communicate, communicate! Tell your customers who you support and why on a regular basis. So much incredible philanthropic work goes unnoticed and under promoted, and some of the greatest value you can offer is awareness. Ask the organizations you support to share the word about your business's commitment and programs that support them, too. The value of broader communications is significant to both your business and the organizations you support. Business philanthropy allows you to reach potential customers who share your commitment to giving back in general or to a specific organization or cause. And at the same time, your business' kindness allows the organizations you support to increase awareness of their work with your audience. It's a win-win for everyone.

A Note on Silent Auctions, Directory Advertising & Sponsorships

As a former preschool silent auction chair, I'm intimately familiar with the pitch: "By donating to our auction, your business will be in front of hundreds of qualified potential customers for your business! And they'll feel great about buying from you because you support the school." Sound familiar? No matter how good the parent volunteer pitch may be, in reality, most families aren't attending silent auctions to seek information on new gyms, jewelry companies or financial advisors. Maybe a few know they want family photos taken and will buy from the photographer who is participating. But the majority will buy what they already know, what they want or what they need to support the school or team hosting the event.

> **"**
>
> Business philanthropy allows you to reach potential customers who share your commitment to giving back in general or to a specific organization or cause. And at the same time, your business' kindness allows the organizations you support to increase awareness of their work with your audience. It's a win-win for everyone.

As for advertising in directories, I'm not a fan unless the organization is compiling the materials themselves. All too often schools, neighborhoods and other groups rely on third parties to assemble content and produce the directories – resulting in your generosity contributing to that company's bottom line rather than the organization you're trying to support. Plus, community members rarely seek out resources in these guides. Directories are used to look up phone numbers and email addresses to coordinate play dates.

Even against this seemingly unsupportive backdrop, this isn't to say you shouldn't participate. While these promotional and advertising opportunities likely won't have an impact on your business objectives, contributing to organizations with which you or your customers have a personal affiliation allows you to demonstrate your support of their goals.

Donate within reason based on what makes you comfortable financially. Your contributions may be in-kind product donations, gift certificates for services, or financial support. Consider what best supports the organization's need and what works best for your business. While a donation can be more affordable than the out-of-pocket costs associated with a sponsorship or advertisement, these can sometimes deliver greater visibility for your business. Again, determine your goals and manage your expectations for outcomes. A bonus – donations of any kind, including sponsorship and advertising of a nonprofit, very often mean you get a tax deduction! Check with your CPA or tax advisor on this, of course, but always ask the organization you're supporting for a receipt.

One final note: Your generosity does not have to be endless. The more philanthropic your business, the more you'll be asked to donate by other organizations. You can choose how many organizations to support, as well as set limits and parameters around donations. Just like company policies and procedures, if explained nicely and clearly, issues are typically limited.

THE BOTTOM LINE

At the end of the day, business is about people. People are inherently good and like to patronize businesses that do good. So embrace your community. Give back to the world. Whether through financial donations or in-kind contributions, advertising or sponsorship, volunteer service or community engagement, a giving program demonstrates your commitment to building the community that supports you. Giving back also empowers your business to connect on a deeper level with your current customers and reach new customers who share your passions.

Section 4

SO, NOW WHAT?
MAKING IT ALL HAPPEN

CHAPTER 23

CHOOSING MARKETING PROGRAMS THAT MAKE SENSE

A new can't-miss marketing opportunity seemingly pops up every day. And when you're looking to grow your business, it can quickly feel like everything you should be doing is too expensive or too complicated. Throw out that notion. There's no one thing that every small business should do or must do to grow. There are no silver bullets. There are many, many marketing tactics available and within reach for small businesses.

Whether engaging with your existing customers or working to reach new ones, money isn't everything. Sure, deep pockets can help make a huge, loud splash. But even small businesses without a huge wallet can reach tons of buyers by focusing on goals and avoiding getting caught up in the "must-do" hype.

What's highly valuable and impactful for one business may fall flat for another. So how do you choose? Start by asking yourself a few key questions – the answers quickly narrow the vast sea of potential marketing opportunities. Then consider budget, your ability to handle growth, and those pesky competitors – we all have them.

ON OBJECTIVES

First, define your objectives for the business, the marketing program and the campaign. Start with your business objective, <u>not</u> the marketing one. Are you working to drive increased revenue from existing customers? Or are you focused on increasing sales of a specific product or from a new audience?

Be specific in your goals – the general notion of increasing brand awareness makes it difficult to measure success. The goal of marketing is to increase revenue. Branding is fabulous and good press is great, but none of it matters if profits don't increase. By starting with goals, you position yourself to make marketing decisions that are grounded in real business results. Keep these business goals in the back of your mind as you map in your marketing goals for each opportunity.

To clarify the difference, when I say "business goals," I mean things like product revenue or client retention rates. "Marketing goals" are things like number of new leads or referrals, hits on a landing page, or entries into a social media contest. Of course you need to convert these leads, referrals, hits or entries into sales for the marketing effort to work. I'll address how to make the most of each program to set it up for optimal success in the next chapter.

With your business goals established, evaluate how they line up with your desired marketing objectives and the potential effectiveness of the opportunity you're considering. More specifically...

Who Do You Want to Reach?

Your Goal: Who are you trying to reach? Existing customers, new partners or new distributors? Be specific! Go back to the ideal customer you defined at the very beginning of this book to ensure you are really clear on your audience for each specific outreach effort. Keep in mind that your audience for a campaign might not include your full target market. Different campaigns serve different purposes and reach different subsets of your total customer set.

The Opportunity: Does this opportunity reach your target market? If you want to reach new customers, does this opportunity help you reach the actual buyer, decision-maker or influencer? Consider not just the raw numbers of prospects, but the specific demographic reached by an opportunity.

"

> The goal of marketing is to increase revenue. Branding is fabulous and good press is great, but none of it matters if profits don't increase.

What Do You Want the Customer or Prospect to Do?

Your Goal: What action do you want the customer or prospect to take? A purchase from your website, a visit to your store, or simply securing an address for your email list?

The Opportunity: Does this opportunity allow your customer or prospect to take action on your desired outcome? Does it give you the ability to engage directly with the customer or prospect to influence the outcome? For example, if your goal is traffic to your website and the opportunity is entirely print based, it may not be a good match.

Answers to these questions help provide a basic framework for go/no-go decisions on opportunities as they present themselves. But this isn't to say that if an opportunity doesn't meet the objectives-focused sniff test above that you shouldn't pursue it.

There are times when you might consider or pursue a marketing opportunity that likely won't help you reach business or marketing goals. You might decide to advertise in a local magazine because your competitors are there and your absence will speak louder than being a part of the mix. Or you might choose to support a friend's new endeavor or a community program for no reason other than because it feels like the right thing to do. That is totally ok! None of these things contradict your customer-centric focus.

ON BUDGET

Objectives are nice, but if you can't afford a program, no matter how perfect a fit it seems or huge opportunity it appears, you simply can't proceed. This isn't a finance book (and I'm the last person to give advice on how much to leverage a business for the sake of growth) but dollars and cents can't be ignored either.

You're not alone in needing to make decisions based on dollars and cents. No small business ever has enough money to undertake every marketing endeavor it wants, needs or could benefit from. In small business, making an impact sometimes requires passion and elbow grease to make up for a shoestring budget. But while most successful small business owners know how to bootstrap their way to growth, as we talked about in chapter 21, sometimes it's simply necessary to spend actual cash to reach an audience, develop materials or attend events.

When you evaluate any marketing or engagement program, consider the full cost of the effort. For example, while having a table at a local event may only be a few hundred dollars, what do you need to make the event a success? Do you need a display, handouts, samples or other tangible materials?

What about staff – do you need to pay team members by the hour to man the table? And on the flip side, what supplies do you already have on hand that can utilize to help reduce the overall expense?

With this full picture of an opportunity's cost, you can better decide if you can afford it or should pursue it. The "should pursue it" aspect of the decision comes from the flip side of cost – the benefits. Using the same local event example, how much new business do you need to bring in for the event to be considered a success? Or, based on your existing conversion rate for new leads, how many new names do you need to collect for your mailing list?

"

In small business, making an impact sometimes requires passion and elbow grease to make up for a shoestring budget.

Also ask yourself what success means to you – dollar-for-dollar break even on the money actually spent? Or is a smaller number ok because you're collecting names for your mailing list and supporting brand awareness? Or perhaps you want to earn a larger return to account for your time spent in planning the event. Only you can decide what "success" looks like for any given opportunity. As with just about everything in this book, there's no wrong answer.

ON GROWTH POTENTIAL

How much growth can you handle? If you're at or near capacity for production, appointments, reservations or service delivery, does it make sense to pursue that campaign right now? If the marketing or customer engagement effort is successful, are you in a position to maintain the same level of service or provide the necessary customer support? Before throwing resources at any program, consider your ability to scale and meet additional customer demand resulting from success.

Even if you're not 100 percent ready to handle the growth today, it may make sense to pursue the campaign anyway. Maybe you're laying the groundwork for a new product offering and are in a position to scale up production when the time is right. Or maybe you have sub-contractors that can help fill gaps if your team is unable to meet immediate demand. Weigh the risks of moving ahead no matter how perfect the opportunity may seem.

Consider the car detailing company that ran a generous offer on a daily deal site but didn't have enough staff and hours in the day to fulfill the appointments before the coupons expired. Eek. Talk about a bad customer experience and lousy first impression. While the campaign could be considered a success because of the number of coupons sold and revenue generated, it was in fact a great failure. In the end, the company couldn't deliver on its promise.

"

There's no one thing that every small business should do or must do to grow. There are no silver bullets.

ON COMPETITORS

As I said earlier in this chapter, there are times when you may decide to advertise in a magazine or attend a community event simply because your competition is there. But as Theodore Roosevelt said, "Comparison is the thief of joy." All too often, small business owners make marketing, pricing and product and service decisions because of comparisons with competitors. Small business owners are often clouded by thoughts of, "If so-and-so is doing it, it must be worthwhile." They question their own rationale or approach based on a fear of missing out (yes, FOMO).

Stop! Stop it now! Focus on your own awesome sauce. Just because your closest competitor is running a sale, adding YouTube to their social media mix, or launching a new service area absolutely does not mean those things are right for you. Even if you offer an identical product or service, you have no idea if they're embarking on a new business strategy, getting out of a line of business, targeting a lower- or higher-end customer, or are in a financial position that demands the marketing shift. Perhaps they're doing something simply because it feels right to them. There's no way to know, and it really doesn't matter anyway.

This is not to say you ignore your competition. You absolutely need to stay on top of what others in your industry are up to. You need to know how you stack up so you can continuously adapt and innovate as your industry changes and customers evolve. But be confident in your choices and that you're doing what's best for your business and your customers.

THE BOTTOM LINE

When evaluating marketing opportunities, there is no right or wrong, must-do or a complete waste of time. Ask yourself these questions to determine if an opportunity is right for you.

- Who are you trying to reach and does the opportunity help you connect with that audience?

- What action do you want your audience to take and does the opportunity allow that to occur or move the customer closer to that action?

- Even if the opportunity doesn't directly support marketing or business goals, do you still have a compelling reason to pursue it?

- Can you afford it?

- Are you equipped to support growth when the campaign is wildly successful?

- Are you considering a program just because competitors are doing it?

CHAPTER 24

MAKING IT HAPPEN: EXECUTING EFFECTIVE MARKETING PROGRAMS

All too often, I hear small business owners gripe that they've tried every possible marketing tactic and nothing works. They're at a loss. They've tried tradeshows and Facebook ads. They've sent newsletters and run sales. Yet business growth is flat. Therefore, they've concluded that their business is just different and traditional approaches or others' best practices seemingly don't make sense for them.

I also hear small business owners cite "brand awareness" as the reason to pursue any number of marketing programs. Yes, brand knowledge is essential for new customers to know you exist, but it's the marketing that occurs after awareness is built that truly drives sales.

In many cases, frustration and underperforming marketing programs come from unrealistic expectations or lackluster execution. For example, too often small businesses go to community events and hand out hundreds of brochures but never follow up with those they meet. And how could they? They had a beautiful banner, but no way to capture contact information for those that came by the table. Or consider the business that turns on Facebook ads to drive traffic to their website, only the website is outdated, confusing and without a clear path for connecting with the business.

> **"**
>
> Brand knowledge is essential for new customers to know you exist, but it's the marketing that occurs after awareness is built that truly drives sales.

So it only makes sense that when these small businesses evaluate whether a program was right for the business or effective at achieving goals, the answer was a resounding no. After all, no new business came from the effort. But again, how could it? The marketing effort was missing some critical keys to success.

Once you've chosen to pursue a marketing program, commit to making it a success. Day-to-day content marketing, special events, pay-for-play advertising, customer love campaigns, or any other marketing program all require the same five key factors for strong execution:

1. *Give customers or prospects a reason to care.*
This might mean finding interesting ways to drive traffic to a tradeshow booth (candy is always a sure winner – who doesn't love year-round trick or treating?) or producing a standout, unique direct mail invitation to a private sale that offers noteworthy savings. Remember that to draw a customer in, you must provide them with clear value.

For example, why should your customers attend your 10th anniversary open house? Just celebrating your business isn't enough for them to reorganize their days. They need more. Give them a reason to care.

2. *Give customers or prospects a reason to remember you.*
Have materials at the ready so customers and prospects have something to reference about your business. For an online campaign, this might be a promotion-specific landing page. For a networking event, it might be nothing more than a professionally produced business card with all of your relevant contact information. Printed material still matters and can provide great value!

3. *Engage and deliver value.*
As I've said throughout this book, it takes more than hanging out your shingle to attract customers eager to buy from you. The same holds true for marketing campaigns. Passing out candy at a tradeshow is only the beginning. Have a conversation with those you meet at an event or that walk into your store. Get to know them and give them the opportunity to get to know you. Give them a few free tips and demonstrate the value that your small business provides.

4. *Give them a reason to buy.*
Bottom line – follow up! Include calls to action, whether in a newsletter, on a postcard or in a print ad. Make clear what action you want a customer or prospect to take, and provide specific instructions on how to take the action. Make sure your website or contact information is front and center. Don't make customers dig.

Another frequent and unrealistic expectation occurs when someone takes your business card, clicks on an online ad, or picks up a brochure. Your work is not done. Be sure to capture contact information or create a path for follow up. Then, actually follow up. Names on a list are the first step, but you need to have a plan for continuing the conversation and closing the sale (or pushing it further along the path toward purchase).

5. Don't forget about awareness.
No effective marketing program works in isolation. Customers need to know what you're up to so they can engage with you! Every content marketing endeavor, in-store event or customer love program can be made more powerful by sharing it across all of your communication channels.

For example, if you're exhibiting at a tradeshow, you can drive increased booth traffic by emailing customers and tweeting before and during the show (use event hashtags!). If you write a blog post, you'll drive more customer views by sharing it via social media and in an email newsletter.

WAIT, WHAT ABOUT THEM?

Even if a marketing opportunity looks perfect on paper and you've mapped out all of the elements for success, step back and consider if your plans consider your customer's perspective. Get beyond the "what's in it for me" and consider what's in it for them. Again, give customers or prospects a reason to care.

Just as you have an endless sea of marketing opportunities, your customers are bombarded with information and marketing messages at every turn. You're competing for their attention and purchases against not only your direct competition but also any indirect substitute. For example, a marketing consultant competes against not only other marketing firms, but also books like this one, workshops, and thousands of blog posts and magazine articles on small business marketing.

Let's go back to something I talked about at the very beginning of the book. Beyond winning the hearts of customers, your marketing campaigns must compete for attention with not only competitor programs, but also every other brand message, life event, and news story out there. Your customers and prospects are parsing your marketing messages alongside the latest viral video on Facebook while getting kids to soccer practice, keeping up with what's happening in the news, and returning a call from their best friend. To be effective, communications, campaigns, offers and follow-up outreach must be compelling to customers and worth their time.

"

Being cute and clever to create intrigue can work if you have major brand power or a big budget to support a campaign, but if you're just building a brand, focus on capturing customers' attention and giving them the information they want and need.

Keeping in mind that while your business is the most important thing in your world, most likely, it's not number one in your customer's mind. So revisit the key elements for success from the customer perspective. Ask yourself – does your marketing message offer something they will care about or remember? Are you interesting or valuable enough for them to commit even the smallest amount of time? And most importantly, will they be compelled to buy or engage?

Alboum Translation Services:
Communicating in the Language of Its Customers

Alboum Translation Services' website and other marketing materials boasted a look and feel that was light years ahead of the majority of its competitors. While competitors were barely differentiated from one another in their flat messaging, stock photography, and outdated web presences, Alboum's design and messaging was clean, fresh, and playful yet professional.

Yet, while Alboum's branding was attractive, it wasn't always resonating with prospects they met at industry tradeshows – the strongest source of leads for the boutique language translation and interpretation company. It wasn't until attendees engaged with Sandra, Alboum's founder and president who rocks events like no other, that they truly "got" the company. Recognizing that they were missing out on leads and opportunities to engage, the small business overhauled its marketing top to bottom.

Look & Feel

Alboum focuses on nonprofits and has specific expertise in public health, tobacco control, education, human services and the environment. To better communicate this niche focus, it moved from maps of the world, graphics of flower petals, and images of happy translators to powerful photography representative of the issues its clients address. The company invested in high quality stock photography for each of the vertical markets it serves. The new images allowed prospects to immediately recognize that Alboum understood their areas of focus and supported their commitment to achieving their mission.

Messaging

Mirroring its approach to photography, Alboum refocused its messaging on demonstrating an understanding of customer priorities and highlighting its translators' experience with customers' issue areas. It also now highlights its notably customer-centric business processes in its messaging. Alboum never charges rush fees or minimums, a common practice in the translation services industry that both frustrates customers and stands in the way of many nonprofits' ability to buy. Alboum's approach makes language translation far more accessible for its nonprofit customers with limited budgets – thereby empowering their abilities to reach greater audiences.

Materials

Recognizing that not all nonprofits are created equal, Alboum moved away from a one-size-fits-none brochure and instead developed content for each industry it serves – applying the images and messaging on industry specific pages within its website and materials for events. While this approach created more work up front, the cost proved no more than going generic.

Recognizing its customers don't like picking up and carrying around reams of printed materials at tradeshows, it produced postcards that contain all the pertinent details as handouts. And it invested in a modular tradeshow backdrop that allows Sandra to customize a single lightweight frame with industry-specific images depending on the show she's attending.

Events

Tradeshows had always been a good source of leads for Alboum, but once the rebranding was done, Sandra turned up the heat on her tradeshow program. She added new events to the mix and went deeper within industries where she'd already seen success.

For example, she attended two new state-level National School Public Relations Association conferences to supplement the success she'd seen at the national conference and the one for the chapter in her home state of Virginia. She went deeper in the public health arena, attending events specifically focused on those who do work in women's and reproductive health – a focus area the company has worked in quite a bit over the years.

Communications

For years, Alboum has sent a monthly newsletter that customers say is engaging, easy to read, and keeps Alboum top of mind. Wins all around! Alboum excels at getting beyond this mass communication, too. Rather than dumping leads collected at tradeshows onto the newsletter mailing list, Alboum follows up directly with each and every person they meet at an event. Sometimes Sandra sends an email and sometimes she sends a handwritten note along with a company-branded notepad. Throughout the year, Sandra keeps in touch with clients by passing along an article or event of interest or sending a quick email just to say hi.

Making It Easy – Simple, Yet Effective Business Processes

While Alboum supports hundreds of clients, translates nearly a million words every year, and has a team of project managers, translators and interpreters, the company lives by a single mantra: "We're easy to work with. We don't have time for complicated and neither do you." To that end, Alboum doesn't require its clients to sign long-term contracts, understand complicated pricing models, or utilize complex technology portals – things all commonplace with its competition. Rather, clients communicate directly with Sandra and her team. Pricing is fair and easy to understand. Documents easily flow back and forth via email.

Building Relationships

"I wouldn't use any other company for my translation projects. Alboum makes me feel as if I'm their only client. I can depend on them completely."

Quite the accolade to receive from a client, eh? But this is just one of many similar client testimonials sharing the same sentiment about Alboum.

There's no formula to Alboum's approach to customer engagement. Engagement happens day in and day out at all levels of the business, from providing excellent customer service to delivering quality work. They are a business that nonprofits want to do business with. While many companies talk about building relationships, it's inherent in Sandra's personality. And it's how she's trained her team. As a result, Alboum has developed relationships with clients and has open lines of communication that many service providers would envy – connections that have been built naturally and over time.

Outcomes

With more than 12 years in the business, Alboum continues to thrive. Sandra is often asked how she has built a business around nonprofits – organizations with notoriously low budgets – and in an industry that is highly commoditized and finding itself butting heads against modern technology (hint: Google Translate is really limited). The answer? Customer relationships and passion for the business. Sandra has committed to being the "agency for the good guys" – empowering those doing good in the world to achieve their missions.

With this focus on her customers, Sandra has built Alboum into a growing business that supports large, global nonprofits and those in her backyard – and also supports her family and fulfills her personally.

Even if an opportunity hits your exact target audience and provides a seemingly great way to connect with a customer, consider whether or not this is where your customer goes to get information about your product or category. Evaluate whether it reaches customers at a time when they're in a mindset to connect with you.

For example, if your ideal customer is busy moms, the family festival in your community might seem like the perfect place to reach them. But moms, who under other circumstances would totally love your offerings, are running between the moon bounce and face painting with three kids in tow. They simply can't take the time to chat. Include an activity at your booth that's enticing to the kids and keeps them busy just long enough for mom to learn a bit about you and provide her email address so you can follow up. Or explore opportunities to provide a giveaway, coupon or marketing material in the swag bag.

When considering the customer perspective, be honest with yourself. Are you actually thinking about what they care about? Be careful that the key messages and calls to action aren't lost. Make it easy. Don't make customers work to get it. Being cute and clever to create intrigue can work if you have major brand power or a big budget to support a campaign, but if you're just building a brand, focus on capturing customers' attention and giving them the information they want and need.

THE BOTTOM LINE

No matter the program, go in with a realistic expectation of your outcome. Whether an effort is 100 percent central to achieving your goals or something less objective–driven, give it every opportunity for success. Ask yourself:

- What creative elements do I need, including any printed materials, website landing pages, advertisements, banners and signs, or even t-shirts or uniforms? How long will it take to create and produce these materials?

- How will I collect customer or prospect information?

- How will I follow up with customers or prospects beyond this campaign? When will I do this? (PS – Carve out time in your calendar.)

- How else can I promote this program?

- Have I considered my customer in my plans? Have I really thought this through from their perspective?

- What help do I need to make all of this a reality? Do I have that help on my team or do I need to find it outside of the business?

CHAPTER 25

SETTING YOURSELF UP FOR SUCCESS

It's no secret that running a small business is a constant juggle. Marketing must be addressed alongside inventory management, new product development, invoicing, hiring and bookkeeping. And those are just the operational concerns. As a small business owner, you must also deliver on the products and services you sell. With so many balls in the air, how can you possibly take the time to evaluate marketing opportunities or execute them to the level of detail I'm suggesting?

There are only two resources in life and in small business – time and money. Perhaps you set aside one day a week or even one hour a day for marketing. Or you develop plans quarterly and then turn them over to employees to make a reality. However, when it comes to marketing (and many other areas of business for that matter), if you can't invest the time, it's worth spending the money. Winging it simply won't work with today's savvy customers.

There's no specific budget of either hours a week or dollars a year I can offer – it's different for every business. It depends on your customer, your offering, your market, your competition and the bottom line. But an investment in business growth can take many forms, and you can be as creative with how you get things done as you like, whether it's relying on employees, consultants, pay-for-play opportunities, or even family and friends. Let's be honest: Most small business owners have asked their kids to stuff envelopes or friends to man a tradeshow booth. Yup – me, too. Guilty as charged. No matter the approach you take, marketing extends your reach as the business owner and enables the essential customer engagement to occur.

"
There are only two resources in life and in small business – time and money.

Whether marketing efforts are large or small, wide reaching or targeting a small subset of customers, commit to doing them well. Make that critical investment of either time or money to position the business and campaign for success. You don't need to wait forever to have each and every detail perfectly defined. However, a program that is rushed or executed just to do "something" rarely delivers.

Likewise, remember that marketing, particularly customer focused efforts, isn't a one-time effort. Tweeting for a day, attending a single networking event, or dropping brochures at a partner business with no follow-up communications won't generate sustained results, build your brand or deepen relationships with customers. For marketing to be successful, it requires ongoing attention and care. Every program, every communication and every act of customer love builds on one another. But the good news is, there are many resources that make great marketing possible! Read on.

Include and Empower Employees.

At the risk of sounding like a broken record, each and every interaction with your business has the potential to impact the customer experience. While the business owner must set the direction and guide the team, every person involved in the business has the opportunity to engage with customers and build relationships. In fact, when everyone on the team has a customer-centered approach, tells the same company story, and delivers excellent customer service, the impact cannot be underestimated.

Your employees (or partners and extended team members) offer a great multiplier for every marketing campaign. Ensure they are aware of a discount you're offering, a push for online reviews you're undertaking or a new product you're launching. With an understanding of the programs, they're in a position to both share the information with customers and support customers seeking to follow up or engage.

Most importantly, embrace your employees and empower them to fulfill your business' commitment to being customer-centric. This means practicing what you preach. Set a good example of showing your customers love and understanding their perspective. Empower employees to engage and communicate with customers, as well as to offer random acts of customer love without asking for permission. The goal is to position your business to offer a consistent, top-to-bottom, customer-centric experience.

Get a Handle on Your Data.

Keeping up with customer information is both a huge undertaking and the easiest thing you can do to empower your customer-centric marketing success. The basics are essential – name, email address, phone number, etc. But details like birthdays, anniversaries, kids' names, and college affiliations are vital pieces of information that truly enable you to create customer love and engage time and again. You can pick up on these personal notes through conversations, sales forms, loyalty program signups, and more. Mostly, it's just about paying attention and writing it down.

The bigger you grow, the more complicated it can be to keep up with all your customer data. But there's no excuse not to! There are tons of tools, programs and applications to help. At Popcorn & Ice Cream, we use Insightly, but this is just one of many customer relationship management (CRM) systems that are free or low-cost; most allow you to scale as you grow. You can even start with an Excel spreadsheet (though I don't recommend it). No matter the system you choose, I recommend getting a system in place as soon as possible and keeping up with it over time. Fair warning: The initial input and organization is time consuming and admittedly painful.

Beyond customer information, keep track of campaigns you send and love you give. Add notes to individual customer records with details of conversations you have or items they purchase. These details further empower your employees to address customer needs, and they support consistency in message and experience because everyone is working from the same background information. Note if a customer came to you by way of a referral from another contact in your network, and add reminders to your calendar of upcoming birthdays and major life milestones.

Last, but absolutely not least, organize your customers and contacts with tags, categories or groups. You might organize by vertical market, demographic set, service purchased, customer source, or networking group affiliation. The goal is to set yourself up to sort customers into groups so you can personalize marketing based on their needs, level of engagement with your business, interest in a topic, or any other criteria.

Use Technology.

Beyond CRM systems, many small businesses use email marketing platforms like MailChimp, Constant Contact or Vertical Response to communicate with customers and prospects en masse, track open rates and manage unsubscribes. Yes! We're total fans. But lots of other tools also empower you to love on customers more easily and keep up with prospects.

Marketing automation platforms are invaluable for streamlining recurring and automated email communications. Services that make personalized snail mail easier also exist. And even though these communications are automated, they don't feel that way to customers when you take advantage of customization options.

You can never replace the genuine connection made with a handwritten note, but in today's connected world, the communications and engagement made possible with technology enables even the busiest small business owners to touch their customers regularly.

Track the Results That Matter.

How do you know if your new customer-centric approach to business and marketing is successful? Sales go up. Existing customers buy again and buy more. New customer inquiries go up. Referrals go up. Close rates go up. These are the metrics that matter. Likes on a Facebook page, free white paper downloads, or samples given away are irrelevant if the business numbers don't follow the same positive track.

Of course you need to watch your website analytics and performance of individual marketing efforts. But if revenues don't rise, something isn't working in the rest of the customer engagement process. So keep an eye on these financial metrics alongside marketing ones. And remember that you want to strike a delicate balance between giving your new customer-centric approach a chance to work and hanging on to programs that aren't driving results. Only you can know what this window for success looks like for your business.

Use Caution and Focus on the Long Term.

It's true in life and in the small business world – if something seems too good to be true, it likely is. Embracing a customer-centric marketing strategy is a long-term commitment to business growth, not a quick fix or revenue generator. I'm not saying you won't see an immediate return when you shift your focus, but be wary of opportunities or ideas that promise rapid, massive results for a small investment. Will they really deliver the kind of customer you want? And watch out for programs or campaigns that bring in deal seekers – often, these customers are quick to move on to the next discount regardless of the customer love you give or engagement effort you attempt.

THE BOTTOM LINE

When focused on running the business, every small business owner struggles to find time to commit to growing the business. So make the most of your marketing programs by setting yourself up for success.

- Invest the time or money necessary to make the program sing.

- Engage employees to help amplify your customer-centric message.

- Keep up with customer information – and leverage it to customize engagement.

- Use technology to make your life easier and simplify program execution.

- Keep an eye on business results. Ask yourself, is this program making a difference?

- Be patient. While small changes can make a big impact, the results don't always occur overnight. At the same time, be willing to pull the plug when programs aren't making the difference you hoped for.

CHAPTER 26

Go!

"Sounds great, Hillary, but where do I even begin?"

Start with a plan.

Once you've made the commitment to becoming a customer-centric business, start with a plan. I'm not suggesting you need to create a fancy slide deck or hire an expensive marketing consultant to get going. But as with everything in business, a plan is critical to success.

The plan starts with stepping back from your business and looking at the entire experience of working with you, buying from you, and even learning about you – from the customer perspective. Look at your business from the outside in. Walk through every customer-facing aspect of the business and identify opportunities that make it easier for customers to engage with you and for you to connect more directly with customers and prospects. Be honest with yourself about areas for improvement – even the most customer-centric businesses can find ways to improve processes and better engage.

In the process of developing your plan, don't forget to focus on the foundation. Putting your best foot forward is critical to every successful customer-centric marketing program.

Get Psyched! Then Slow Down.

Be excited about marketing! Then, temper that drive and do one thing at a time. I'm hopeful after reading this book that you'll be bubbling over with tons of great ideas for your business. But attempting to implement all of them at once will almost certainly result in as much frustration as you had with previously underperforming marketing efforts.

Start with one new program at a time. Determine how you'll engage deeper with customers, roll out the effort, make it a part of your business processes, implement systems that enable consistency, and review effectiveness. Once the program is humming along, keep it in place as you move on to add the next component.

Go Off Script.

While planning is essential and the details matter, don't wait until each and every detail is ironed out and perfect before you move forward with engaging your customers. Many small business owners are perfectionists and want every detail of every marketing effort to be perfect. I get it – I totally get it. I'm right there with you. But while this is great and demonstrates a commitment to excellence, it can also hold you back.

Take the story of the premium stationery distributor who made a great connection at an industry tradeshow with a designer who was very interested in working with her. The distributor held back on following up because she didn't have her new website finalized or brochure printed and ready to mail. She was missing out on a great opportunity due to a desire for perfection. But the designer was intrigued without the pretty marketing materials. What mattered was the connection. The distributor didn't need to wait to implement her new follow-up strategy to move the relationship forward. And if she had waited, she would have missed out on a great opportunity. The distributor called the designer, set a meeting and now the two enjoy a great partnership.

When a customer commitment is part of the fabric of a small business, great engagement comes naturally. Engagement can't be forced or overly scripted – customers are quick to sniff out the difference between a company that truly cares and one that's simply marketing. This is another area where being small is a huge asset – you don't need to run ideas up the food chain or secure multiple approvals – you can love on your customers whenever it makes sense.Oftentimes, it's the unplanned engagement that deepens customer relationships the most.

"

When a customer commitment is part of the fabric of a small business, great engagement comes naturally. Engagement can't be forced or overly scripted – customers are quick to sniff out the difference between a company that truly cares and one that's simply marketing.

Review Your Plan Regularly.

Just as your company evolves, so do your customers. This evolution happens whether you're growing or staying the same size consistently year over year (which isn't always a bad thing). Remember that the goal of your customer-centric approach is to deepen relationships and get customers talking about you. The only way to continue to do this is by continuously surprising and impressing them. If you run the same marketing and engagement programs year over year, they become expected. While consistency and knowing what to expect from a company is great, you also want to continue to excite your customers with the new and unexpected.

Stop Complaining.
"My business is harder, because…"
"My industry is just different, because…"
"My situation is more complicated, because…"

As small business owners, these things are easy to say. They're easy to believe. I constantly hear small business owners convincing themselves of all the reasons it is more difficult for them than their fellow entrepreneurs.

All small business is hard. What's actually hard isn't the business, the industry or your life. It's the work. Being an entrepreneur takes hard work. You will experience ups and downs. Businesses do not grow themselves. Being an entrepreneur takes motivation, dedication and gumption. That's the reality of business. The excuses? Those are the easy part.

Talking ≠ Growth
Committing to a customer-centric focus, reading a great book, attending an inspiring workshop or developing exciting plans are all awesome steps toward great marketing and business growth. But those steps are just talk. You must walk the walk, too. Great ideas have to move to actual execution and implementation for them to be effective. Embracing and engaging your customers takes time and hard work.

So put time in your calendar to focus on it – even if that means talking to employees, consultants, or other vendors who make your marketing ideas a reality. Spend time on marketing and customer engagement each and every week. Build a steady drumbeat of "We Love Our Customers" and let that inspire your communications, decisions and actions.

> **"**
> **All small business is hard. What's actually hard isn't the business, the industry or your life. It's the work. Being an entrepreneur takes hard work.**

Be Excellent.

Walt Disney said, "Whatever you do, do it well. Do it so well that when people see you do it they will want to come back and see you do it again and they will want to bring others and show them how well you do what you do."

I couldn't agree more. Bottom line – at your core, your offering must be strong. And you must be consistent in your customer experience. Your product must perform well, your store must offer fair pricing and a great experience, and your services must deliver as promised and then some. At the end of the day, no amount of marketing can save a bad product, service or shopping experience. And no single "wow" experience will sustain indefinitely.

Embrace the Challenge.

Before you dive in, take a step back. Sit in awe of everything you've already accomplished. Remember why you started your business in the first place. Recognize that you already have customers that adore you. Embrace the business you love. When you start by reminding yourself of your passion, ideas, and motivation, the success will come.

THE BOTTOM LINE

You can do this. By reading this book (and making it this far!), you've already taken a HUGE step toward loving your customers.

So go forth and conquer. There's tons of business out there to be had and growth to be achieved. Make it yours!

With hugs, confidence, appreciation and customer love,

Hillary

THANK YOU. THANK YOU.

Many books contain thank yous and acknowledgements. Now, having been through the writing process myself, I truly appreciate the meaning and passion behind those pages. To say I couldn't have done this without the support of others is the understatement of the century.

To each and every small business owner: Thank you for believing in your dreams. The world is a better place because of your inventions, your perspectives and your visions. I love my work and am excited to head out every morning because of you. Forget about the best companies to work *for*, I'm honored to work *among* the best companies in the world: Yours.

To Jack Mitchell: I stumbled on *Hug Your Customers* as an Amazon recommendation and will forever be grateful to the targeting that led me your way. You are an inspiration. I've often called *Hug Your Customers* my "Bible." I recommend it to many a small business owner and often send a copy as my hug to them. Thank you for your leadership and vision.

To Amy, Emma, Alston and Monika: Thank you for getting my vision and helping to make it a reality. This book wouldn't be here without any of you. Your talents are unmatched and I sing your praises daily.

To Mom and Dad, Mom and Dad, Lindsay, Rachel, Jaime, Nicole, Alissa, Julia, Rachel, Meghan, Sandra and (in the words of many Academy Award winners) the many others who know who you are: Thank you for your encouragement and confidence. Thank you for listening over and over to me say, "I need to get this done. I'm going to get this done. I want to get this done." Thank you for being proud of me.

To Scott, Sammy, Jack and Isaac: Last but certainly not least – another phrase I understand now far better than before embarking on my journey as a business owner – you support me in ways that can't be put into words. You believe in me and encourage me. Most importantly, you love me. And I know that isn't always easy. I couldn't do it without you and wouldn't ever want to. In the words of Grandma Kay, all my love, with all my heart.

A PERSONAL NOTE

I love small businesses. I love seeing an entrepreneur turn a flicker of an idea into a profitable business. And I love watching passionate people turn their talents into high-demand products and services. I'm inspired by dreamers and motivated by doers.

In 2011, I started Popcorn & Ice Cream to provide small businesses with marketing strategy on a scale appropriate to their businesses and at a price they could afford. I took my years of marketing experience and chose the path few other MBAs do – I went small.

Every small business owner has a story, a tale of why they started their business and what led them down the path of entrepreneurship. And I'm no different. I'm not just a small business consultant – I'm a small business owner, too. Here's my story.

When my husband Scott started his independent financial planning business, he needed assistance defining his brand, his marketing communications, and his client service model. As the resident marketing expert in our house, I went out to find the right consultant to help.

I quickly found many excellent and creative freelancers, but I could not find someone to point him in the right direction on how to best leverage these talented graphic designers, copywriters, web developers and photographers. I came up empty as I searched for a consultant to provide advice on which branding materials to create, marketing tactics to pursue and client engagement models to implement.

At the time, I was entrenched in my marketing career at a mid-sized Washington DC agency. I oversaw multi-million dollar public relations and marketing budgets for Fortune 500 companies, managed multiple teams, and enjoyed an admittedly nice salary for someone who was barely 30 years old.

My unsuccessful effort to find a consultant for Scott left me with a choice – help him hire an in-house marketing manager or do the work myself. I chose the latter, and I count it among the best decisions of my life.

I had my "resume-builder clients," the impressive, immediately recognizable big company names in my personal portfolio. But the clients I truly loved were the smaller businesses and startups, whose projects no one else wanted because their budgets were small and challenges were large. These were the clients that got me out of bed in the morning. It was time to take my experience at a failed dot.com (essentially Facebook, but before its time), at the startup network security company (later acquired by a major telecom), and with the agency's smallest clients and apply my expertise to something more personal – the business that would become the primary source of income for my family.

While working alongside Scott to build his business, I started researching how to build my own. I chatted with many small business owners about their marketing challenges, and I found that many got stuck in the same places. They didn't know how to effectively communicate what they offer, how to stay connected with existing customers, and how to reach new audiences. And they told me that they consistently struggle to sort out which marketing tactics make the most sense for their specific businesses amidst a sea of social media platforms and advertising opportunities. I discovered these challenges weren't unique to the type of business, industry, or number of years in business.

That's why I founded Popcorn & Ice Cream. I wanted to work with small businesses and support their goals for growth, brand building and engagement. The goal of all small business marketing should be to increase revenue. Branding is fabulous and good press is great, but none of it matters if profits don't increase. Without being anchored by business goals, marketing is just noise.

Additionally, I knew that while the tactics that work for big businesses are both inappropriate and unaffordable for most small businesses, the same underlying principles apply.

This book, *Customer, LLC*, is the next evolution of this vision. With this book, I want to make truly relevant marketing strategies available to businesses of all sizes. That means we will look at what other small businesses are doing, not what the Apples and Zappos of the world are doing. Plus, the need for more impactful marketing is more real than ever. According to the Small Business Administration, only 50 percent of small businesses last more than five years. And even fewer make it to the 10 year mark.[8] Yes, some close up shop because they discover that business ownership just isn't for them, but for many, it's a matter of dollars and cents. Without sufficient growth, maintaining the business won't support your day-to-day financial needs – or allow you to support your family.

Thank you for reading and sharing my passion for customer-centric businesses. And thank you for embracing customer service and building a business that I'd be excited to patronize. Finally, as a fellow small business owner, thank you for building a broader small business community we can all be proud of and for inspiring customers to shop small and buy local.

I hope this book sparked great ideas for generating customer engagement in your business. Please write to me at customerllc@popcorn-icecream.com and let me know how this book inspired you. By sharing your story, you inspire me, too.

ABOUT THE AUTHOR

Hillary Berman is passionate about small business and customer-centric marketing. She is the founder of Popcorn & Ice Cream – a Washington DC-based marketing consulting firm that focuses exclusively on small businesses and startups. A graduate of Syracuse University's S.I. Newhouse School of Public Communications and the University of Maryland's Robert H. Smith School of Business, Hillary can also be found building lemonade stands with her three budding entrepreneurs at home.

REFERENCES

CHAPTER 6
1: Leggett, Kate. *Trends 2016: The Future Of Customer Service.* Forrester Research, Inc., 2016.

CHAPTER 9
2: Farris, Paul, Neil Bendle, Phillip E. Pfeifer, David J. Reibstein. <u>Marketing Metrics: The Manager's Guide to Measuring Marketing Performance (3rd Edition)</u>. Pearson FT Press, 2015.

3: Webber, Alan E. *B2B Customer Experience Priorities In An Economic Downturn: Key Customer Usability Initiatives In A Soft Economy.* Forrester Research, Inc., 2008.

4: *Yodle Insights: What Consumers Want from Local Businesses.* Yodle Web.com, Inc., Web.com Group, Inc., 2015.

5: *Yodle Insights: What Consumers Want from Local Businesses.* Yodle Web.com, Inc., Web.com Group, Inc., 2015.

CHAPTER 12
6: *BrightLocal Local Consumer Review Survey 2015.* BrightLocal, Bright Little Light, Ltd., 2015.

CHAPTER 13
7: Goodman, John. *Manage Complaints To Enhance Loyalty.* Quality Progress, 2006

A PERSONAL NOTE
8: *Frequently Asked Questions.* U.S. Small Business Administration, 2014.

Index

F

G

H

I

K

CPSIA information can be obtained
at www.ICGtesting.com
Printed in the USA
LVOW11s1017260317
528500LV00001B/181/P